JANE AUSTEN

JANE AUSTEN

A BRIEF LIFE

FIONA STAFFORD

YALE UNIVERSITY PRESS
NEW HAVEN AND LONDON

For information about this and other Yale University Press publications, please contact:

U.S. Office: sales.press@yale.edu   yalebooks.com
Europe Office: sales@yaleup.co.uk   yalebooks.co.uk

Set in Adobe Garamond Pro by IDSUK (DataConnection) Ltd
Printed in Great Britain by TJ International Ltd, Padstow, Cornwall

Library of Congress Cataloging-in-Publication Data

Names: Stafford, Fiona J., author.
Title: Jane Austen : a brief life / Fiona Stafford.
Description: New Haven : Yale University Press, 2017. | Includes
    bibliographical references and index.
Identifiers: LCCN 2017019450 | ISBN 9780300232219 (alk. paper)
Subjects: LCSH: Austen, Jane, 1775–1817. | Novelists, English—19th
    century—Biography.
Classification: LCC PR4036 .S73 2017 | DDC 823/.7 [B] —dc23
LC record available at https://lccn.loc.gov/2017019450
A catalogue record for this book is available from the British Library.

10 9 8 7 6 5 4 3 2 1

CONTENTS

Introduction	1
Childhood	11
Early Writing	29
The True Art of Letter-Writing	43
Bath	59
From Home to Home	73
Sense and Sensibility and *Pride and Prejudice*	87
Mansfield Park and *Emma*	105
Persuasion	127
'Winchester Races'	139
Remembering Jane	147
Afterword	153
Notes	167
Bibliography	171

INTRODUCTION

'What did she say? – Just what she ought, of course. A lady always does.' When Emma finally discovers Mr Knightley's true feelings, after forty-eight chapters of misunderstanding, the relief is almost overwhelming. At last, perfect happiness is in prospect, and the joy that arises from the page is all-encompassing. Any sympathetic reader must share the pleasure of the moment when the barriers crash down and the truth is revealed at last, though there is still a sense, even then, of something withheld. Confusion may be gone, but control is not. The tact with which Jane Austen preserves her heroine's privacy, while inviting readers to participate in her intense delight, is characteristic of her mature novels. Of all writers, she is the most adept at creating both characters who seem to possess an independent existence *and* a narrator to whom readers feel able to turn, as if to an intimate friend.

Emma's reply to Mr Knightley, which is 'just enough' to prompt him to say more himself, is typical of her creator's method. Jane Austen frequently offers the kind of detail that encourages her readers to allow their imaginations free rein, without issuing a subsequent rebuke. *Northanger Abbey* more or less requires readers to imagine a suitable husband for Elinor Tilney, when the narrator, conscious of 'the tell-tale compression of the pages' that signals the story's imminent ending, announces that any detailed delineation of Elinor's husband is unnecessary because 'the most charming young man in the world is instantly before the imagination of us all'. As so often, we are left knowing everything – and nothing. Austen's narration is at once intimate and elusive, inviting and retreating. No wonder, then, that so many readers over the years, who have responded to the promise of her fiction with such gratitude, have also felt a certain curiosity about the woman behind the works.

When it comes to Jane Austen's own life, the same enticing balance between intimacy and distance is apparent. We know exactly where she lived and died, and when and where she wrote her great novels. She is surrounded by a virtual forest of family-trees, with the first-hand recollections of her various relations providing the starting point for any biographical research. We can identify her friends and the circles in which she moved, the homes she visited, the parties she attended. Letters survive from Austen herself, packed with details about bonnets and brooches, guests and gooseberries, donkeys and dinners, sewing, sicknesses, even something of her reading. Compared with many writers living two centuries ago, we know a great deal about Jane Austen. And yet, there is still an extraordinary elusiveness about her life. Even though the first biography was written by her brother within months of her death, our knowledge of Austen seems minimal in the areas that really matter – her methods of composition, literary opinions, political views, religious beliefs and, above all, emotional attachments. There is some evidence relating to each of these important areas, but, all too often, the surviving details seem to throw up as many puzzles as they solve. Like Mr Knightley in the shrubbery, Austen's biographers seem to receive just enough from their object of fascination to make them want to say more.

Every reader feels that, in some sense, he or she knows Jane Austen. The engaging tone of her narration, the quick truths and the deep understanding of human nature are all so distinctive that we seem to recognise her clear voice instantly. Hence the confidence with which so many have been quick to create their own images of the author. But, whether speculation about Jane Austen by her immediate and extended family, or by later enthusiasts, scholars or film-makers, comes close to the original truth is impossible to determine. 'Seldom, very seldom, does complete truth belong to any human disclosure; seldom can it happen that something is not a little disguised, or a little mistaken.' Jane Austen may have had Emma Woodhouse in mind when she wrote this, but it serves as a suitably witty warning to anyone attempting to narrate her own life. The kindness with which Emma's misunderstandings are ultimately treated nevertheless suggests that Austen herself might have derived amusement rather than alarm from the efforts of her followers, appreciating that any biographical endeavour is always inspired by the intangible attractions of her novels. Her own practice as a writer was to set out situations or introduce characters with remarkable economy, leaving the task of drawing out the likely consequences to her readers. It is perhaps appropriate, then, to consider not only the known facts about her life, but also some of their implications.

As soon as the novels are seen not as autonomous worlds, peopled by their own distinct cast of characters and internal rules, but rather as the compositions of a real woman in a particular place and time, questions spring up about the relationship between the life and the writing. Indeed, once it dawns on us that Jane Austen's life spanned one of the most turbulent periods of world history – the American War of Independence broke out when she was six months old, the Bastille was stormed when she was thirteen, war between Britain and France went on almost uninterrupted throughout her adult life, and she died within two years of Waterloo – the silence of her novels on such matters comes as something of a surprise. She was a wartime novelist and yet her writing conjures up worlds in which all the important action takes place on the dance floor, in the drawing room or around the garden. During Austen's lifetime, Britain experienced massive social and economic transformation, with new industrial and agricultural methods of production, urban growth and improved systems of communication developing under the rule of an unstable king and dissolute prince. Uprisings in Ireland, riots in England, victories and losses abroad, political union, the assassination of a prime minister – all took place while Austen was writing. None of these public events seem to make much impact on her apparently realistic novels. Why not?

It is not just the absence of contemporary political references that proves a puzzle for readers, however. Once the focus shifts to Austen's own immediate experience, the gap between what is known of her life and what is apparent in her fiction is again clear. Apart from short visits to friends and family, thirty-four of her forty-one years were spent in the English county of Hampshire, yet none of her novels is set there. She grew up in a household of six boys and two girls, but she created families of daughters – the Dashwoods, the Bennets, the Woodhouses, the Elliots. Only two of her heroines have an elder brother, even though Jane Austen had five. Her father was rector of the parish where she was born, but her most memorable clergymen are absurdly vain, self-seeking figures. She lived with her mother until her own death, but her protagonists' mothers are deceased, absent or distinctly unhelpful. The Austen family suffered its fair share of illness, death and difficulty, but none of those circumstances quite matches the problems depicted in her fiction. Jane Austen never married, and yet each of her novels adopts the traditional resolution of comedy and fairy tale, moving towards it with unswerving conviction.

What are we to make of this? How can we make sense of Austen's life and art? At a time when most women received so little formal education and none could obtain a place at university, how did Jane Austen come to write books that have commanded the attention of some of the most brilliant minds ever since? Why were these the novels that Charles Darwin knew by heart, that Alfred, Lord Tennyson preferred over seventeenth-century political history, that Winston Churchill read during the Blitz? Such questions require more extensive answers than a short biography can hope to provide, but they are worth considering at the outset because so much of Austen's public persona is still hidden under the modest exterior presented by her siblings and preserved by her Victorian nephews and nieces. This brief life has no interest in tearing down the images of Jane Austen that have been created by numerous earlier admirers and iconoclasts – images to which each new biographer is so greatly indebted. It is, however, propelled as much by the puzzles as by the biographical evidence, and is sustained throughout by an undiminishing sense of wonder at the fact of Austen's fiction.

A book of this kind incurs many debts. The first major critical assessment of Jane Austen's work appeared during her own lifetime, shortly after the publication of *Emma*. It was written by a literary giant, Walter Scott, and published in a leading journal, the *Quarterly Review*. Scott's encomium was followed all too soon by Henry Austen's brief biographical notice of his much-lamented sister, which accompanied the posthumously published *Northanger Abbey* and *Persuasion* in December 1817. Jane Austen's reputation then grew intermittently and, by the later decades of the nineteenth century, it was so well established that there was no danger of her novels receding into oblivion. The writer whose books were first attributed to an anonymous 'Lady' has gradually attracted an almost overwhelming share of the literary-critical limelight, and so this account of her life and work owes much to those who have contributed to the Austen illuminations. The main written sources are listed in the bibliography, but the book has also benefited from opportunities to spend time in the places Jane Austen lived, visited and set her stories, especially Bath, Box Hill, Chawton, Lyme Regis, Portsmouth, Steventon and Winchester. I am indebted to the generous curators of the Jane Austen's House Museum, Louise West and Mary Guyatt, as well as to Gillian Dow and her colleagues at Chawton House. Vivian Branson's kind invitation helped me to understand Jane Austen's family connections in Kent, and I have been privileged enough to meet a number of contemporary descendants of the extended Austen family. The Jane Austen Society, including several regional branches, has always been very welcoming, and I have learnt a great deal from my many enjoyable interactions with its members. I am also glad to be able to discuss Austen with students and colleagues at Oxford, including Ros Ballaster, Paula Byrne, Sandie Byrne, Richard Jenkyns, Freya Johnston and Kathryn Sutherland. Once again, I have been very fortunate to work with the excellent editorial team at Yale University Press, and thanks are due especially to Melissa Bond and Julian Loose for their enthusiasm and expertise. I would also like to record a special debt of gratitude to Clare Alexander.

As with so many real lives, Jane Austen's did not conform perfectly to the narrative patterns that inform her novels.

The reason that she is the subject of this and so many other biographies is that she wrote six fine books. Since they were all published in the space of six years, between 1811 and 1817, this brief life is shaped accordingly. If the number of words and the number of years represented do not seem to match, it is because Jane Austen's greatest achievement was packed into less than a fifth of her life. Though rarely placed in the company of her brilliant contemporaries, Jane Austen was just as much the Romantic genius as Keats, Burns, Shelley or Byron – full of youthful exuberance, intensely creative once she had found her individual voice, and dead before she reached middle age.

CHILDHOOD

---◆►█◄◆---

1775–87

There are not many babies in Austen's novels. Late in *Pride and Prejudice*, Mr Collins brings news of a 'young olive-branch' that will make the Bennet family's eventual loss of Longbourn complete, while in *Emma*, the child to be born at Randalls is perceived by the heroine as the final stage of Mrs Weston's removal. Young mothers tend to be kept largely at a distance from the action or used for purely narrative purposes, as when the news of Mrs Price's desperation over 'her ninth lying-in' sparks the storyline of *Mansfield Park*. Although we have glimpses of a more kindly attitude in Emma's drawings of her baby nephew, or in Mr Palmer's secret fondness for his son and heir in *Sense and Sensibility*, no young child emerges as a fully rounded character in any of Austen's novels. Judging from comments in her own letters, Austen's views on birth were decidedly mixed. Though a much-loved aunt, her private opinion of the frequent pregnancies of her own niece Anna Lefroy suggests that successive children were not always greeted with delight: 'Poor Animal, she will be worn out before she is thirty. I am very sorry for her.'[1]

Austen herself had no children, and nor did her sister Cassandra. Neither did she have much opportunity to play with baby siblings from an early age, unlike so many children of her time. Her eldest brother, James, for example, had the experience of seeing five young baby boys and two little girls appear in his mother's arms by the time he was fourteen years old. For Jane, however, the only younger brother was Charles, who arrived when she was three. Mrs Austen's practice was to send her babies to be nursed in the village after their first few weeks at home, and so, among young Jane's earliest memories might have been the arrival and subsequent departure of little Charles. By the time she was ten, her glamorous cousin Eliza de Feuillide and her baby son Hastings were frequent visitors at the Austen family home, but the little boy's serious health problems meant that he was always a focus of protective anxiety rather than a spring of pure delight. It was not until the next generation of Austen children began to arrive, with the birth of her nieces Fanny and Anna in 1793, that Jane had much close contact with babies – by which time she was seventeen and more preoccupied with other plans of her own.

Jane Austen grew up surrounded by big boys. Born at Steventon parsonage in Hampshire in December 1775, she was the seventh child of the local rector, George Austen, and his wife Cassandra. When Jane arrived a month late, during one of the hardest winters of the century, Reverend and Mrs Austen were already the parents of James, George, Edward, Henry, Cassandra and Francis. The arrival of another child was therefore not as momentous as births often seem, even though this baby would eventually become one of the most remarkable writers in the English language, the popularity of her work ensuring lasting fame for the entire family. As the youngest girl, Jane inevitably developed a sense of herself in relation to her elder brothers, to whom she turned at different times for advice, amusement, company and comfort. The boisterous household meant that her early life was never quiet, dull or lonely, but it must have provoked the occasional disappointment, frustration and feeling of inadequacy, as large families invariably do. Among siblings, deep affection and aggravation generally go hand in hand. The reassuring closeness may also have brought dim fears of insignificance – little Jane mattered very much, but still she was only one of eight. As a child, Jane Austen must always have felt that there was someone a bit older and wiser than her, both providing a model and also, no doubt, piquing her into proving her own ability.

When it came to talents, after all, her family was not underendowed. Her eldest brother, James, born in 1765, was bright, energetic and widely read. He hunted and wrote poetry with equal enthusiasm, a combination of interests less surprising then than now. Edward, three years younger than James, was good-looking and good-humoured, with a steady head and a talent for telling amusing stories. His younger brother Henry, handsome, clever and rich in optimism, livened up every gathering with his effervescent humour and sparkling conversation. Cassandra, the first daughter, born in 1773, was eighteen months younger than Henry, but more like Edward with her dark beauty, kind nature and quiet intelligence. Francis, who arrived a year later, was active and determined from the start, as is evident in the story of him buying a pony at the age of seven to enable him to go hunting with his older brothers. Francis was the first Austen to go to sea, and ended up as Admiral of the Fleet, the highest-ranking officer in the entire British navy. Charles, the baby of the family, born in 1779 and growing up to be just as intelligent, good-tempered and courageous as the rest, followed Francis into the navy in 1791, just before France declared war on Britain. Only George seems to have missed out. The second son, born just a year after James, was destined to become something of an exile from the family hearth. From childhood, he suffered from fits, speech difficulties and an unspecified mental disability, which led to him being fostered by a nearby family and largely edited out of the Austen family narrative.[2]

As a child, Jane Austen was part of a family that provided all the security of connection and continuity, but also instilled an awareness of separation and perpetual change. With such lively relations, there was constant amusement, intellectual stimulation and companionship, but only very rarely would everyone have gathered under the same roof. The span of fourteen years between the births of the oldest and youngest Austens meant that James was already setting off for Oxford in the year that Charles was born. George's strange exclusion must also have heightened his sister's sense of the lottery of human existence and the fragility of her own place in a world in which one child could be blessed with grace and ability and another with neither. Gratitude for good health and natural gifts, as well as compassionate understanding of those afflicted with difficulties, formed part of Jane Austen's psyche from her earliest years – and informed the novels she would write in later life.

In addition to George's absence, she also had to contend with some abrupt departures. When she was only eight, Edward was adopted by a wealthy, childless relative of their father, one Thomas Knight of Godmersham Park in

Kent. From Mr Knight's point of view, his action was very generous: relieving his second cousin from the expense of educating at least one of numerous sons, and guaranteeing the boy a secure future with a gentleman's estate and social standing. Unlike Francis and Charles, who had to earn their place in the world by entering a dangerous profession and working hard to impress their commanding officers, Edward's prosperous future seemed to have appeared from nowhere. It was a reward for nothing more than a healthy constitution and his position as a younger son (though not too much younger). Once again, the arbitrary but profound differences in people's lives must have made a deep impression on his sister. The wrench of separation also demanded strategies of psychological self-defence, contributing, perhaps, to a fear of relying too heavily on even those who were most dear.

When Frank followed Edward out of the family home in 1786 to train as a naval officer, the same feelings of loss were compounded by anxiety. The hazards facing a young midshipman did not require as vivid an imagination as Jane Austen's to provoke the most profound fears, and so, when the twelve-year-old boy went cheerfully away to serve king and country, his sister must have wondered whether she would ever see him again. Mustering a proper pride in Frank's courage and sense of patriotic duty demanded considerable effort in such circumstances. By the time Charles emulated Frank's example in 1791, the fifteen-year-old girl was faced with an even harder task of waving off her little brother into military service just before the outbreak of a war in which naval battles were to prove crucial to the British campaign.

Not all the fraternal exits were quite so traumatic, however. James and Henry both went up to Oxford and came home safely and frequently. James and Edward both enjoyed extensive continental travels, returning unscathed and full of news of foreign countries. The return of any of the sons was a major event at the parsonage, not only bringing the natural joy of reunion, but also a vital infusion of ideas and stories from beyond rural Hampshire. For, although Steventon and the surrounding parishes were full of other large families with their own share of births, marriages, deaths and human incidents, there were inevitably times when the tiny village seemed rather quiet. The cycle of the seasons created the natural pattern of the year, while the church calendar guided the regular services given by Reverend Austen and attended by his family. Life at the Steventon rectory was measured by the annual Christian festivals – Epiphany, Lent, Easter, Whitsun, Trinity, Michaelmas, Advent and Christmas – as well as being marked by the yearly challenges of the farm and field: ploughing, drilling, lambing, haymaking, harvesting, partridge-shooting and foxhunting.

In a rural community, the vagaries of the English weather are particularly important, and, since George Austen had a farm to run, as well as full responsibilities as a minister of the church, the conditions determining good and bad harvests were more than just a matter for conversation. For a little girl, however, the changes in the seasons mainly brought different clothes and activities. During the cold and dark winters, once the excitement over the beauty of frosted cobwebs or a sudden deluge of snow had faded, it must have seemed a lifetime before the days started to lighten and last longer again. Sewing samplers, reading books and playing games could pass the time quite happily, but anything that broke into the frozen months between October and March was very welcome indeed.

When James, the pioneer of journeys into the wider world, came home for the vacation in 1782, he threw himself into amateur dramatics. Oxford had put him in touch with contemporary fashions, and one of the enthusiasms sweeping eighteenth-century England was the vogue for private theatres. The Steventon rectory might not have been as capacious as some of the country houses in which miniature versions of London playhouses were being installed, but it had a sizeable parlour and a barn, so why not a makeshift stage? Unlike the Bertram family in *Mansfield Park*, the Austens were fortunate in having parents who encouraged their children's creative talents, and thus constituted an audience rather than an obstacle. Mrs Austen may have been given to spending time on the sofa, like Lady Bertram, but she was also a very lively woman with a real facility for witty verses, sharing a delight in wordplay and comedy with her children. George Austen was a highly educated man, a fellow of St John's College, Oxford, before his marriage, and he remained keen to maintain his wide intellectual pursuits and literary enthusiasms, as well as to nurture the budding ability of the next generation. In order to help make ends meet as his family increased in size, he offered rooms and private tuition to young gentlemen. Often his pupils went home in the holidays, but those who were still in residence provided the possibility of a larger cast for the family theatricals. Among the earliest productions at Steventon was a tragedy called *Matilda*, in which Thomas Fowle, a residential student who would later propose to Cassandra, read the epilogue. Mostly, however, the plays offered opportunities for the Austens themselves to showcase their talents and have a lot of fun.

It must have been very exciting for Jane to watch her elder brothers performing Sheridan's hilarious comedy *The Rivals*, which had first been staged at Covent Garden in 1775, and to be introduced at such an early age to the memorably muddled Mrs Malaprop and to the imaginative world of Lydia Languish, which so completely eclipsed the real one. Jane was both an integral part of the family and an eager observer, by virtue of being too young to be given a role. She would have enjoyed the final production, but also have witnessed the hours of preparation that went into such an ambitious play – the boys learning lines, rehearsing scenes, setting up props and developing stage accents. To produce a convincing fiction for a single evening, vast effort, time and co-operation were required. But it was well worth it, for here was a chance to delight a sympathetic audience, make people laugh and demonstrate personal abilities. The plays at Steventon gave James Austen the opportunity to recite his own compositions alongside those of the best playwright of the age – a thrilling idea for his exceptionally talented little sister. On the stage, new identities could be assumed, and anything seemed possible – a point especially evident in *The Rivals*, in which the actor cast as Jack Absolute had to play Jack playing Ensign Beverley. Jane would have been laughing, but also learning, because the very idea of a pretend persona was out of the question in the kind of community where everyone had known everyone else since birth. This was a world complete in itself, operating according to the playful internal logic of Sheridan's drama. The theatre at Steventon, though only a family affair, demonstrated to the younger Austen children just what art could mean, even in the most confined and remote places.

The scripts chosen by James for family performances offered both entertainment and education. For the young Jane Austen, however, observation of the human interactions during rehearsals must have been just as instructive. One person's eagerness to dominate the stage, another's reluctance to participate, endless disputes over casting – all the details that are so well observed in *Mansfield Park* were in evidence at Steventon during her childhood. When Eliza de Feuillide entered the scene for the Christmas production of 1786, the atmosphere intensified as the usual tiffs and reconciliations took on a decidedly flirtatious edge.

Eliza was the daughter of George Austen's sister Philadelphia, who had taken the bold decision to risk a long sea journey and tropical climate when she set off for India in 1752. Once landed, she met and married Tysoe Hancock, giving birth to Elizabeth eight years later. When Eliza returned to Europe and married the French aristocrat Comte de Feuillide, she called their son Hastings after her godfather, Warren Hastings, Governor-General of India and close friend of her parents, especially Philadelphia. Whether Warren Hastings was in fact the little boy's grandfather has often been debated, though the evidence on either side is patchy. Whatever Eliza's parentage, she certainly made an exotic addition to the male-dominated household at Steventon when she swept in to stay for extended visits during the 1780s. Brought up in India, she was familiar with lands that the Austens had only read about. Married to a French count, she had moved in circles they had only imagined. With her young son and distant husband, she seemed both vulnerable and emancipated. Though some years older than all her Austen cousins, she was young enough and beautiful enough to seem very exciting indeed.

Eliza was prepared not only to join in the family shows, but even to take the leading role in comedies, which meant that the scope for plays – and playing – increased significantly. The epilogue James wrote for Susannah Centlivre's comedy *The Wonder*, which Eliza delivered in the 1787 production, is basically a celebration of women and their new freedom from male tyranny:

> But thank our happier stars, those days are o'er,
> And woman holds second place no more.
> Now forced to quit their long held usurpation,
> These men all wise, these Lords of the Creation!
> To our superior rule themselves submit,
> Slaves to our charms, & vassals to our wit;
> We can with ease their every sense beguile,
> And melt their resolutions with a smile.[3]

It was quite a change for the Austen brothers, and a startling shift of emphasis for the little sisters. If James was quick to admire Eliza, Henry was even more beguiled by his captivating cousin, and their enjoyment of each other's company was obvious to everyone. Eliza was ten years older than Henry – and married. However, by 1797, when he reached twenty-six, she had been left a widow and was therefore free to become his wife.

Jane's cousin introduced an entirely new kind of woman into her mental horizons. Unlike Mrs Austen and so many of their family friends, Eliza seemed free to arrive when she wanted, stay as long as she liked and then disappear again, apparently unencumbered by household management or parental restrictions. In reality, Eliza's life was far from easy: distress over her husband during the French Revolution and anxiety for their invalid son took their toll. From young Jane's perspective, however, here was a woman who had seen the world, who spoke French as easily as English, who dressed fashionably and brought Parisian manners to rural Hampshire. She was also fond of her English relations, remaining close to Jane and Cassandra as they grew into womanhood, teaching them things that would otherwise have been well outside their experience.

If Eliza was an exciting addition to the circle, however, it was Cassandra who formed its centre as far as Jane was concerned. Her brothers came and went, leaving havoc in their wake, but Cassandra, Jane's only sister, remained a constant, vital source of stability throughout her life. The sisters shared a bedroom, a sense of humour and a mutual understanding that sustained them both throughout their lives. Though rarely apart, even as adults, whenever they did find themselves staying in different places, they wrote frequent letters to each other, as if to deny any thought of separation. From their earliest days, Cassandra was Jane's guide and confidante. As all the family recognised, the girls were everything to each other. It is not surprising, therefore, that the first heroines to appear in Jane Austen's published works were also sisters. Jane's attachment to Cassandra was such that, when it was deemed time for Cassandra to receive a more formal education than she was being given at home, Jane was determined to go too. Even though she was only seven, boarding school with Cassandra was better than home without. As her mother commented at the time, 'If Cassandra were going to have her head cut off, Jane would insist on sharing her fate.'[4] In the event, the joke turned rather sour, as both the girls were lucky to survive their schooldays.

Departure from the family home was not, after all, an exclusively male experience. Jane and Cassandra, together with their cousin Jane Cooper, daughter of Mrs Austen's elder sister, set off for Oxford in the spring of 1783 to be educated by Jane Cooper's aunt Mrs Cawley, who was the wife of the principal of Brasenose. The ancient city was also the home of their uncle Theophilus Leigh, Master of

Balliol and subject of endless college anecdotes. James Austen was there too; like his father before him, he had become a fellow of St John's. None of this was especially heartening, however, for a seven-year-old girl away from home and surrounded for the first time in her life by the unfamiliar sounds and smells of a city. Mrs Cawley, with her formal manners, would not have seemed much of a substitute for Jane's mother and father, and the exclusive company of little girls could not have been more different from that of the Austen boys. If Jane had been close to Cassandra before, she now clung to her elder sister for comfort and companionship amid the 'dismal chapels' and 'dusty libraries' of the medieval seat of learning.[5]

The summer of 1783 was dark and alarming. Gilbert White, who wrote the famous *Natural History* of the Hampshire village of Selborne, recalled the unprecedented heat and humidity, the plagues of wasps and the rotting honeysuckle. Even worse were the terrifying meteors, thunderstorms and 'smokey fog' that covered the whole of Europe for weeks, 'a most extraordinary appearance, unlike anything known within the memory of man'.[6] We now know that the cause of these startling phenomena was the massive volcanic eruption of Skaptár-Jökull in Iceland, but for those witnessing them in England in 1783, the disasters seemed biblical in proportion and mysteriousness. For Jane and Cassandra Austen, the strange summer must have been very frightening indeed, but their fears were compounded by the outbreak of illness at Mrs Cawley's establishment, which led to their sudden removal to Southampton.

The journey from Oxford to the great port on the south coast was slow and tiring, but, upon reaching Southampton (well known for its mild air and healthy sea breezes), the girls would be safe. Or this, presumably, was Mrs Cawley's plan. In fact, the city was soon afflicted by an epidemic of typhus, which spread alarmingly in the unusually hot summer weather. Despite the danger, Mrs Cawley continued to superintend her charges and decided not to inform their parents, even when both Jane and Cassandra fell seriously ill. It was Jane Cooper who broke the news and, within days of her letter arriving, Mrs Cooper and Mrs Austen were hurrying down to Southampton to collect their children. Jane and Cassandra slowly regained strength at Steventon during the autumn, but Mrs Cooper, who had become infected during her rescue mission, did not survive.

Despite the experiences of 1783, the Austens decided to send their daughters away again two years later, this time to what is now the Abbey School for Girls in Reading. Although the school was part of a ruined abbey, where ghosts reputedly walked and where skeletons were certainly uncovered from time to time, the experience seems to have been generally happier than Jane's first foray into formal education. Under the slightly eccentric but kindly guidance of Mrs Latournelle, with her distinctive cork leg, Jane and Cassandra practised their spelling and handwriting and learned some basic French and Italian, as well as acquiring other specifically female accomplishments such as needlework and drawing. They also had access to different books in the school library and to very different company in the classroom. Here was an opportunity to make friends independently of the family and to learn about the various ways in which schoolgirls interact, form close allegiances, compete, console, embrace and exclude one another. Mrs Latournelle's pupils came from other towns and villages, talked of unknown homes and families, held unfamiliar ideas about the world and different hopes for the future. Although Jane Austen was only in Reading for two years, completing her formal schooling by the time she was eleven, her mental field of vision had already widened immeasurably. All her new experiences, deeply mixed as they were, were laid down to ferment in her rich imagination.

EARLY WRITING

1787–92

Although Jane Austen was not at school for very long, her education extended far beyond what was offered by Mrs Cawley and Mrs Latournelle. As Elizabeth Bennet explains to Lady Catherine de Bourgh, even without schooling or a governess, those who 'wished to learn, never wanted the means'. In *Pride and Prejudice*, Elizabeth's quick wit and elegant choice of words are not attributed to the kind of formal education deemed appropriate for young ladies, but rather to her intellectual freedom – 'We were always encouraged to read.' Once back at home, Jane Austen was similarly at liberty to explore the books owned by her parents and her brothers and to learn from her family's wide reading and educated tastes. James, in particular, with his love of poetry and classical literature, helped to encourage his sister's literary flair before his marriage to Anne Mathew in 1792. Not only was James eager to discuss literature, he was also keen to write. In addition to composing prologues for the family theatricals, James wrote elegies and sonnets in the style of contemporary poets such as Shenstone and Bowles, eventually attempting reflective blank verse along the lines of Cowper's poem 'The Task'. Equally fashionable, if very different in tone, were James's charades, which reflected his mother's comic tastes and aptitude for riddles. When Mr Elton produces his verse puzzle in *Emma*, he is following a model familiar to Jane Austen since childhood.

James's poetry remained unpublished, circulating only among the Austen family. In 1789, however, with the help of his younger brother Henry, he launched himself on the public at last with *The Loiterer*. The title was an obvious gesture towards the highly successful literary journals of the day, Dr Johnson's *The Idler* or Henry Mackenzie's more recent publication, *The Lounger*. Oxford-based and Oxford-oriented, *The Loiterer* appeared every Saturday for over a year, offering – what the editor promised in the first issue – 'moral lectures, critical remarks, and elegant humour'.

For Jane Austen, now thirteen, the paper also provided a chance to see some of her own words in print. In the ninth issue, published on 28 March 1789, James included a letter from an anonymous female correspondent, complaining about the male bias of *The Loiterer* and demanding new contributions 'from among the young of both sexes'.[7] Although the authorship of the letter, which was published under the name 'Sophia Sentiment', has never been established absolutely, it seems more than likely that the editor's young sister had a hand in it – indeed, she may well have written the entire piece. The playful tone and the parody of sentimental tastes is certainly in accord with Jane Austen's earliest surviving writings, while the entertaining suggestion for a moving tale has much in common with her 'Plan of a Novel', composed in response to correspondence with the Prince Regent's librarian many years later, following the publication of *Emma*. In the letter, Sophia Sentiment requests 'some nice affecting stories, relating the misfortunes of two lovers, who died suddenly, just as they were going to church'. The comic conciseness of the sentence, with its abrupt juxtaposition of the clichéd and the unexpected, is as typical of the young Jane Austen as the plot summary that follows:

> Let the lover be killed in a duel, or lost at sea, or you may make him shoot himself, just as you please; and as for his mistress, she will of course go mad; or if you will, you may kill the lady, and let the lover run mad; only remember, whatever you do, that your hero and heroine must possess a good deal of feeling, and have very pretty names.

Jane may not have written the whole letter, but parts of it seem unmistakably hers.

The letter from Sophia Sentiment is important not only as the first published work of Jane Austen, but also because of its subject matter. Though obviously related to contemporary debates over female education and appropriate reading for girls, Sophia Sentiment (whose name means 'wise opinion', as well as being a parody of the silly fictional heroines of the day) is also a sign of changing attitudes at Steventon. The insertion of a female perspective into the male conversation of *The Loiterer* reveals much about developments within the Austen family in the 1780s as the younger children began to make their own voices heard. As Jane entered her teens, she was only too conscious of herself as a girl, with feelings and expectations that were very different from most of her siblings. She benefited enormously from the knowledge, advice and encouragement of James and Henry, but obviously recognised that she had her own views, especially when it came to literature. What's more, she was eager to express them.

Jane Austen's early writings were carefully preserved by her family after her death, and so, although they were not published until the twentieth century, the three little volumes now provide a rich resource for any reader interested in her work. The pieces she composed between 1787 and 1792 show the early growth of her astonishing literary talent and the way in which it was fostered by her own sense of an immediate audience. Almost every story, poem or playlet is a present to one of her family. 'The Three Sisters' is for 'Edward Austen Esquire', 'The Visit' is dedicated to 'the Revd James Austen', 'The Beautiful Cassandra' to 'Miss Austen', and 'Sir William Mountague' to 'Charles John Austen Esquire'. Some of the creations are offered for a specific purpose, such as 'Frederic and Elfrida', which was given to her close friend Martha Lloyd as 'a small testimony of the gratitude I feel for your late generosity to me in finishing my muslin Cloak', or the two little tales 'Jack and Alice' and 'The Adventures of Mr Harley', which were for Frank, now far away and serving as 'a Midshipman on board his Majesty's ship the Perseverance'.[8] Writing was a way of expressing love and friendship, even if both were apparently being mocked in the stories themselves. 'A Letter from a Young Lady, whose feelings being too Strong for her Judgement led her into the commission of Errors which her Heart disapproved' includes Anna Parker's confession that she murdered her father very early in her life and has since murdered her mother, before concluding with the resolution, 'I am now going to murder my Sister', but this does not mean that Jane's parents and Cassandra did not enjoy the little spoof just as much as they were meant to. The miniature comedies depend on the improbability of their narratives and the way in which the familiar is suddenly transformed into something surreal. They also demand an audience who understands the joke.

At every turn, the restrained language of polite eighteenth-century literature is disrupted by unexpected action and often violence. In 'The Beautiful Cassandra', for example, the eponymous heroine falls in love with a particularly pretty bonnet her mother has been making for the 'Countess of ——'. Taking the bonnet, Cassandra sets off to make her fortune, curtseying to the first young viscount she meets, before going on towards the bakery. At this point, the comedy explodes:

> Chapter the Fourth
> She then proceeded to a Pastry-Cooks where she devoured six ices, refused to pay for them, knocked down the Pastry-Cook and walked away.[9]

At twenty-three words, it is not a long chapter, but its effect on the mini-novel is overwhelming. What begins as a parody of contemporary sentimental fiction suddenly introduces a moment of slapstick violence, conveyed with extraordinary verbal economy. The young writer observes the acceptable modes of contemporary writing and behaviour with great astuteness, but is also constantly alert to the possibilities of the unlikely and the unacceptable.

Throughout the early writings, Jane Austen's delight in creating little worlds in which anything can happen is abundantly evident. In 'Henry and Eliza', the fairy-tale detail of the baby discovered in the haycock sets the scene for an extravagant romantic adventure, but its traditional elements are balanced by the distinctive comic outlook that marks so much of Austen's work. When Eliza finds herself imprisoned in Newgate by her persecutor, 'the Dutchess', her response is more reminiscent of Emma Woodhouse than of Cinderella: 'No sooner had Eliza entered her Dungeon than the first thought which occurred to her, was how to get out of it again.'[10] After spending a few weeks working through the bars on her cell window, her escape is hindered by anxiety about her children's safety on the descent down the prison wall. She is, however, a resourceful heroine, and, after some (fairly rapid) deliberation, she arrives at a solution: 'At last she determined to fling down all her Cloathes, of which she had a large Quantity, and then having given them strict Charge not to hurt themselves, threw her Children after them.' Eliza is both a fairy-tale character and a believable young woman in an unbelievable situation.

Despite the wildness of Austen's imaginary incidents, these buoyant stories are generally grounded by numerous details of recognisable human characteristics, turns of phrase or familiar places. Mr Clifford, for example, is introduced through a catalogue of his many carriages ('of which I do not recollect half. I can only remember that he had a Coach, a Chariot, a Chaise, a Landeau, a Landeaulet, a Phaeton, a Gig, a Whisky, an italian Chair, a Buggy, a Curricle and a wheelbarrow'), but he then spends five months laid up in the 'celebrated City' of Overton, the town nearest to the Austens' home at Steventon, where he is cured by the 'no less celebrated Physician'.[11] In other stories, the perspectives of different characters are brilliantly caught, such as that of the postillion in 'Frederic and Elfrida', whose 'stupidity was amazing' because he declares, 'without the least shame or Compunction, that having never been informed, he was totally ignorant of what part of the Town, he was to drive to'.[12] The scale and scope of the early pieces may be modest compared with the novels of Austen's maturity; their ambition, however, is anything but. Though the narratives are brief, or sometimes straining to run away, they are lit by brilliant flashes of observation and by numerous dazzling sentences in which not a word is wasted.

Austen's juvenilia reveals a young writer in the process of self-discovery and a young reader eager to master anything that may come her way. She experimented with a remarkable variety of genres, producing playful imitations of contemporary novels, scenes from Restoration comedy, comic operettas and conduct manuals, and even composing a short history of England. In every piece, she is in dialogue with established writers, learning from their example, but also daring to take exception to their practices and views and to put forward her own, highly individual, position. The comments she scribbled in Goldsmith's *History of England* reveal a vivid imaginative engagement with his account of the English past, as she laments the fate of Christopher Layer, hanged, drawn and quartered for his support of Ormond – 'Poor Man! Alas Poor Man' – or as she responds to the detail of Cromwell's massacre of Drogheda – 'Detestable Monster!'[13] Imaginative reading was the prelude to imaginative writing and, when Jane Austen turned her hand to British history, her own account was just as full of sympathetic involvement with figures such as Elizabeth Woodville, 'who, poor Woman!, was afterwards confined in a Convent by that Monster of Iniquity and Avarice Henry the 7th'.[14]

Everything Jane Austen read came alive, but, at the same time, her natural empathy with those she encountered through her reading was kept in check by a keen sense of the ridiculous and of the potential absurdity of emotional display. When Charlotte reflects on the unfortunate predicament of her double engagement in 'Frederic and Elfrida', for example, her suicidal plunge is treated with lightly: 'She floated to Crankhumdunberry where she was picked up and buried.' Austen even composes a comic epitaph in the manner of contemporary commemorative tablets:

Here lies our freind who having promis-ed
That unto two she would be marri-ed
Threw her sweet Body and her lovely face
Into the Stream that runs thro' Portland Place.

Austen's love of literary form and her delight in the comic potential of language would always prevent her sympathetic nature from emanating as sentimentality on the page. The girl who chose to give her pastoral heroine, Chloe, a song in which she yearns for Strephon to carve the partridge, 'if it should be a tough one. / Tough one, tough one, tough one . . .', would never allow her pen to dwell in the regions of simple romance.[15] When Jane Austen presented Jane Cooper with an elaborately alliterative dedication, she signed herself 'your Comical Cousin'. In her early writings, she was not only developing her literary skills, but also learning to define herself.

As a young writer, Jane Austen wanted to find out what she could do. As one of the youngest in a large family, she also wanted to show everyone else what she had found out. Making people laugh was a way of making them listen. For, although her miniature novels were often written for her closest companion and most sympathetic reader, Cassandra, much of her early writing seems to have been designed to impress as well as to entertain. One of the most substantial pieces, which must have demanded considerable authorial effort, is 'Love and Freindship', dedicated to her cousin Eliza. As if to bridge the age difference between the young author and her patroness, who was now turning thirty, the little epistolary tale begins as the heroine reaches fifty-five, and is assumed by her younger correspondent to be safe at last 'from the determined Perseverance of disagreeable Lovers and the cruel Persecutions of obstinate Fathers'. Fifty-five-year-old Laura is less convinced that the time for adventures is over, but nevertheless agrees to unfold the story of her life so far, in a series of letters that effectively parody every cliché of the contemporary literature of sensibility.

Some of the earliest pieces were for Jane's parents. In 'The Mystery', she humbly solicits the patronage of her father, in a dedication that is parodic but still expresses a child's desire for parental approval. As the youngest daughter, Jane probably had to work quite hard to attract attention from her busy parents, and so her talent for creating amusing stories was a very happy discovery. Though younger than her brothers, and educated according to the expectations of an age in which women of her class were meant to marry and have babies rather than pursue an academic education or a profession, Jane Austen's natural ability and determination enabled her to surpass her literary siblings from a very early age. To the great credit of her parents, they encouraged rather than curbed her genius, and so the dedications of her early compositions convey a genuine debt of gratitude, as well as mockery of contemporary literary fashions.

Despite Jane Austen's early discovery of the possibilities of the page, her writings also reveal an awareness of potential limitation. The earliest surviving pieces offer playful miniaturisation of contemporary literary styles, with 'Amelia Webster', for example, providing a diminutive example of the epistolary fiction popular at the time. Here, Austen managed to introduce three different couples and conclude with their marriages in the space of the seven very short letters that fly between the various characters and the unknown observers, Tom and Jack. 'Edgar and Emma', a slightly more substantial narrative in the third person, depicts the return of Sir Godfrey and Lady Marlow to their family seat after an absence of two years and its profound effect on their daughter, Emma, who has been nursing a passion for Edgar Willmot. Emma's discovery that, of all the numerous Willmot children (the list runs to more than twenty), Edgar is the one away at college produces a powerful reaction: '[S]he remained however tolerably composed till the Willmot's were gone when having no check to the overflowings of her greif, she gave free vent to them, & retiring to her own room, continued in tears the remainder of her Life.' Although the comic excesses of the tale are beautifully handled, it offers an alternative ending to the happy unions that so quickly bring closure to 'Amelia Webster'. Even at the age of twelve, Jane Austen was aware that there seemed only two possible endings for a young woman's story – either marriage or melancholy isolation. Her tales show an early, and remarkably assured, sense of the way narrative works, as well as an awareness of the limited choices allowed by society to women, whatever their natural ability.

By 1792, the comic energy of her tales was as vigorous as ever, but her writing also reveals a growing interest in human situations and prospects. In 'Catharine', for example, the sentimental heroine's refuge in her favourite bower provides both the centrepiece for parodying contemporary literary convention and a space for more serious reflection on the fate of those who had helped create the shady arbour – the Wynne sisters. Catharine's close friends had lost their parents and therefore their home and financial security. As a result, one was now 'splendidly, yet unhappily married', while the other, 'scarcely more comfortable', had been employed as a companion to the daughters of a dowager.[16] The story begins by reducing two young women to lives of misery, which leaves the bereft Catharine to an uncertain future at the mercy of her aunt and neighbours. The author's acute perception of the precariousness of human life, and especially of young women's fortunes, gives the unfinished tale an edge that is quite different from the extravagant freedom of some of the earlier pieces. At sixteen, Austen was alert not only to the ways in which fictional narrative works, but also to the less manageable stories of real men and women.

As Edward and James married and set up homes of their own, the pressure to find a suitable partner was beginning to bear upon the younger members of the household. While Jane Austen was imagining the future of Catharine in her bower, her cousin Jane Cooper was being swept away in a whirlwind romance and marriage to a handsome captain in the navy. When Revolutionary France declared war the following February, Henry enlisted at once in the Oxfordshire Militia. Charles was already at the Royal Naval Academy in Portsmouth and would soon follow Frank into active service at sea. For Jane Austen at seventeen, the prospect of eventually being left alone in a large house with ageing parents was beginning to seem threatening to a degree that could not be entirely dispelled.

THE TRUE ART OF LETTER-WRITING

1793–7

When Catherine Morland tells Mr Tilney that 'one day in the country is exactly like another', she is reflecting the experience of a young woman whose life until the age of seventeen has been spent in 'a small retired village' and who now finds herself amid the bustle and variety of Bath. In 1797, at the age of twenty-one, Jane Austen visited the fashionable spa town for the first time. The fear and excitement of being jostled in the crowded assembly rooms and thronging streets went straight into the novel she began to write upon her return to Steventon. Unlike Catherine, however, Jane Austen had already realised that Bath's attractions, considerable as they were, could not necessarily eclipse the appeal of rural life. Tiny villages and elegant towns both had their merits, however different in kind.

What *Northanger Abbey* demonstrates is that, by the end of the 1790s, Jane Austen was in a position to recreate either setting within the pages of a novel, and to develop fictional voices capable of presenting opposing points of view with complete conviction. The difference between her work at the beginning and end of the decade is remarkable, and even though nothing she completed during this period was published within her lifetime, it represents a crucial stage of Jane Austen's development, both as a writer and as a woman.

Although Catherine Morland might not have noticed much going on before her arrival in Bath, life at Steventon was full of drama. If the outbreak of war transformed Henry Austen into a tall, scarlet-coated lieutenant, it also placed him in potentially mortal danger, itself deepened by his own determination to obtain a commission in the regular army rather than the militia. Even his posting in the militia saw him rapidly sent off to Southampton to defend the realm against the very real threat of a French invasion. Hampshire, a county on England's south coast, whose harbours accommodated the principal naval ports of Portsmouth and Southampton, was on the front line of any imminent attack: if the Revolutionary forces were victorious, the area around Steventon would be one of first to fall into enemy hands. Nor were the fears generated only by newspaper reports of distant political developments. In the summer of 1794, Jane's cousin Eliza returned to the rectory, traumatised by her experiences in France and full of overwhelming memories of what she had witnessed. She had reached Calais, heavily pregnant, given birth to a baby, who had died almost at once, and then escaped across the Channel. On top of the distress and physical upheaval, she had to contend with the thoughts of her husband's trial, the hostile evidence given by their own servants, and his death on the guillotine. Eliza had grown up in India and travelled across half the world, but nothing had prepared her for the shock of a familiar European country convulsed in revolution.

If Eliza's experiences in the 1790s were bound up with the great historic events of the period, other members of Jane Austen's family were experiencing things that might not register publicly but were just as momentous personally. The marriages of Edward and James were followed a year later by the births of their children Fanny and Anna, giving Jane and Cassandra new identities in the family – as aunts. James, his wife and daughter moved into the rectory at Deane, within a mile of Steventon, where James had become the curate and worked under his father's guidance. Little Anna would never remember her mother, however, for James's wife Anne died suddenly in May 1795. Within two years, he had married again, choosing for his bride Mary Lloyd, who was not to prove the easiest stepmother for his daughter, though she swiftly provided a son and heir to carry James's name and genes into the next generation. As James planned his second wedding, Eliza also readied herself to exchange widow-hood for marriage to her long-standing admirer Henry Austen, now old enough to seem a suitable partner and full of just the kind of optimistic energy to help renew her hopes and happiness.

Cassandra, too, seemed destined to escape her role as sister, daughter and aunt, for she had become engaged to Thomas Fowle, former student at the rectory, now ordained as a clergyman and hoping to establish himself in a satisfactory living. If Jane's delight in her sister's happiness was tinged with some private dismay at the thought of their permanent separation, she was still quick to sympathise with Cassandra when it emerged that, instead of an early wedding, Tom Fowle would be disappearing overseas for many months. When asked to accompany his uncle, Lord Craven, across the Atlantic as the chaplain on board his ship, Tom agreed to go. With Frank and Charles already in the navy, the Austens knew all about the hazards and discomfort of long voyages, and were only too aware of the likelihood of a hostile confrontation with an enemy fleet. In the event, Tom suffered not from the French, but from a fever, dying in St Domingo in 1798 before he and Cassandra had the chance to marry.

Upheavals such as these at home and abroad must have had their effects on all concerned. And what was Jane Austen doing during the tumultuous 1790s? She seems to have spent most of her time dancing. 'I fancy I could just as well dance for a week together as for half an hour,' she wrote on Christmas Eve, 1798, capturing the mood of the night before and of much of the preceding decade.[17] It is not until January 1796 that modern readers get a proper glimpse of the young Jane Austen, speaking in her own voice to the person closest to her. Her earliest surviving letter to Cassandra was written at Steventon over a January weekend, when Jane was twenty and her sister was celebrating her twenty-third birthday with her fiancé at the Fowles' family home in Kintbury, not far from the market town of Newbury. Her birthday greeting is just as light-hearted as the compositions she had given Cassandra in the past, hoping that her sister would 'live twenty-three years longer',[18] before moving swiftly on to the real treat – an account of the previous night's ball. After detailing the various members of the party, she admits, teasingly, 'I am almost afraid to tell you how my Irish friend and I behaved.' The details are withheld with just the same control that she would later exert on the narration of her novels, and just the same encouragement to let the mind race on: 'Imagine to yourself everything most profligate and shocking in the way of dancing and sitting down together.' Whatever the pleasures of Kintbury, some part of Cassandra must have been eager to know more about her sister's evening with her 'Irish friend', Tom Lefroy.

Jane's Tom lived in Ireland, but had spent Christmas visiting his relatives at Ashe, a village close to Steventon and Deane. Jane was especially fond of Mrs Lefroy, and so found herself attending the same balls as Mrs Lefroy's nephew and evidently enjoying his company very much, despite meeting him on only three occasions. Though apparently sanguine about his imminent departure (which would leave 'nothing to console us till the arrival of the Coopers on Tuesday'), she describes him as 'a very gentlemanlike, good-looking, pleasant young man' and, towards the end of the letter, admits that he had 'but *one* fault . . . that his morning coat is a great deal too light'.[19] The detail is really an excuse for Jane to compare Tom Lefroy to Henry Fielding's impulsive, hugely attractive, but decidedly dangerous, fictional hero ('He is a very great admirer of Tom Jones') and to convey to Cassandra some of the excitement of their profligate and shocking conversations.

Five days later, she wrote again to mark the day 'on which I am to flirt my last with Tom Lefroy', adding: 'My tears flow as I write, at the melancholy idea.'[20] Her language recalls the sentimental heroines of her early parodies, and shows that her command of exaggerated emotional expression could be usefully applied in the management of her own feelings. If Cassandra doubted her tone for a moment, she would have been reassured by the very next sentence announcing that William Chute had called the day before, which includes a typical comic touch: 'I wonder what he means by being so civil.' It is hardly the letter of a broken-hearted damsel, but it does convey very powerfully the sense of a young woman enjoying life, discovering her own sexual feelings and recognising that she herself is poised for adventures in the adult world.

Throughout her twenties, Jane Austen's letters are filled with news of balls and ball-gowns. Though she wrote to Cassandra only when they were apart, and even some of that correspondence was destroyed, the surviving letters give a vivid sense of Jane Austen's life and opinions as a young woman. The 'true art of letter-writing', she observed on 3 January 1801, is 'to express on paper exactly what one would say to the same person by word of mouth'.[21] Reading her letters to Cassandra thus gives us the privileged sense of eavesdropping on their conversations. Their close relationship meant that Jane could express her feelings freely, in terms that she knew would be understood and received with kindness. Following a Christmas ball in 1798, she was riding on a cloud of warm memories after dancing all twenty dances of the night: 'My black Cap was openly admired by Mrs Lefroy, & secretly I imagine by every body else in the room.' Merely a fortnight later, things turned out rather less happily: 'I do not think I was very much in request – People were rather apt not to ask me till they could not help it.'[22] Personal disappointments nevertheless afforded comic opportunities, and so the very good-looking officer, who had apparently been so keen to meet her, is despatched in her letter with easy wit: '[A]s he did not want it quite enough to take much trouble in effecting it, We never could bring it about.' The voice is irrepressibly lively, even amid the most challenging of social minefields. If she was disappointed by Tom Lefroy's failure to visit her when he stayed with his aunt in November 1798, some three years after their flirtation, the letter that refers to the matter betrays little visible sign of distress, carrying on with typically witty observations on Mary (who would be 'glad to get rid of' her rheumatism, and her child) and Mrs Portman ('not much admired in Dorsetshire; the good-natured world, as usual, extolled her beauty so highly, that all the neighbourhood have had the pleasure of being disappointed').[23] It is not that Jane Austen lacked deep feeling, but her favourite mode for letters, as for every other kind of writing, was comic.

Although it is possible to detect in her private corre-spondence some of the emotional upheavals experienced during the 1790s, the surviving letters also bubble with excitement over new experiences, revelations about human nature, flirtatious conversations and hopes of even better encounters to come. They suggest a young woman who is keen to share her experiences and observations, but who is always writing primarily to entertain an affectionate reader. When she arrived in London in August 1796, for example, she reached at once for pen and paper, adopting a familiar parodic tone to convey her obvious relish of the great city: 'Here I am once more in this Scene of Dissipation & vice, and I begin already to find my Morals corrupted.'[24] Three years later, when she travelled to Bath, the same air of excitement runs through the account sent to Cassandra, but this time there are more witty comments on those she had encountered, like Dr Hall, who was 'in such deep mourning that either his Mother, his Wife, or Himself must be dead'.[25] The apparent suppression of sympathy in observations of this kind is really an expression of feeling for someone who mattered more to her than Dr Hall, and who would recognise the tone of the sentence instantly. Jane Austen's references to death and disease were very often pithily phrased, as if to emphasise the comic absurdity of the human condition when its most vulnerable aspects were being exposed.

She wanted to make Cassandra laugh – just as Cassandra's letters pleased her. We no longer have the letters sent by Cassandra, but numerous references in Jane's correspondence suggest that they were a source of great enjoyment: 'The letter which I have this moment received from you has diverted me beyond moderation,' she wrote on 1 September 1796, 'I could die of laughter at it, as they used to say at school.' Cassandra's fine letters set high standards, and Jane responds by calling her 'the finest comic writer of the present age' – a compliment reminiscent of the extravagant dedications in her early writings, but also indicative of Jane's own values and aims.[26]

Occasionally, the letters do reveal her anxieties, as in the one despatched on 18 September 1796 from Edward's home at Rowling in Kent. It begins with a confession that the morning has been spent 'in Doubt and Deliberation' and ends with a rare, but telling, apology: 'How ill I have written. I begin to hate myself.' Throughout the letter, her uncertainty about how she was going to get home to Steventon undermines her determined comedy, giving her joke about falling into the hands of 'some fat Woman who would make me drunk with Small Beer' an uncomfortable edge. Letters such as this afford a sharp insight into Jane Austen's utter dependency on her relations and her own fundamental lack of freedom. Generally, her writing offered a world in which she was in command, but here the pressure of a situation that rendered her powerless to make decisions was disrupting the smooth control of her prose.

Although Jane Austen spent so much of her young adulthood planning her wardrobe and enjoying parties, writing remained crucial to her sense of self and general well-being. Her first surviving novel demonstrates the care that she devoted to her creative work during the 1790s and the continuing force of her experimental spirit. *Lady Susan* is a remarkable transitional text, retaining all the irreverence of her earliest work, but also revealing many of the strengths of her maturity. It is designed to startle readers – and a glance through the responses it has elicited over the years shows that it has been very successful in this respect. Though epistolary in form, the fictional letters in *Lady Susan* are most unlike those written by Jane to Cassandra: they are used to construct distinct characters who are often shown to be motivated by a self-seeking desire to influence their correspondents. When inviting herself to her brother-in-law's house at the start of the novel, for example, Lady Susan is a model of politeness and propriety, but to her admirer, Reginald, she presents the tones of passionate indignation. Only Mrs Johnson is allowed to read about her friend's calculated manipulation of everyone she encounters, but even those letters seem chiefly designed to show off Lady Susan's secret triumphs to a less successful woman of the world.

The discrepancy between Lady Susan's fond references to her daughter, Frederica, in the opening letter to Mr Vernon and the subsequent assessment sent to Mrs Johnson – 'She is a stupid girl, & has nothing to recommend her'[27] – could hardly be more marked. Jane

Austen is revelling in the possibilities of language, revealing that words are as prone to deceive as to denote the truth. Lady Susan is a brilliant writer who knows the power of a good narrative: 'I trust I shall be able to make my story as good as her's. If I am vain of anything, it is of my eloquence.' Though she has struck many readers as a monster of amorality, she is also, in part, a fantasy figure for a young woman whose own life offered so few real choices and whose chance for personal autonomy depended on her imagination and skills as a writer. Lady Susan's 'desire for dominion' and love of 'universal admiration' may be despised by her sister-in-law, Mrs Vernon, but they reflect something of the author behind the fiction, who seems to have used her novel to start exploring some of the complexities of the human psyche and of the relations between different people. In this case, a woman who, despite her fading beauty, could command the desire of every man she encountered, and whose primary means to control her world were linguistic, had an attraction that extended beyond the eyes of her fictional suitors. At the same time, the abhorrence of Lady Susan that is manifest in so many of the letters suggests an acute awareness of the potentially unappealing nature of eloquence and of the dislike so easily generated by an intelligent woman, who could be deemed cunning, unmaternal or coquettish. Lady Susan is at once attractive and repulsive, and the choice of the letter form allows conflicting responses to exist side by side.

The satirical comedy of *Lady Susan* seems less exaggerated than that of Austen's earlier writing because the characters are more developed and the situations more realistic, but the novel is still full of similar jokes. Lady Susan's dismay at being forced to visit 'that insupportable Spot, a country village', is clearly meant to amuse the Austen family, as is her observation that 'I have never yet found that the advice of a Sister could prevent a young Man's being in love if he chose it.' It is also easy to hear Jane Austen's enjoyment of verbal economy in Lady Susan's advice to Mrs Johnson on the management of husbands: '[S]ince he will be stubborn, he must be tricked.' Integral to the humour, however, is a more serious concern with human behaviour and social codes. The novel gave Jane Austen an opportunity to air some of her exasperation with contemporary notions about the education of girls, as Lady Susan despatches her daughter to a fashionable boarding school despite believing that being 'Mistress of French, Italian, German, Music, Singing, Drawing &c will gain a Woman some applause, but will not add one Lover to her list'. Frederica's desperate escape from the school and the subsequent revelation of her fondness for independent reading is more than a joke at her mother's expense. It suggests Jane Austen's own dissatisfaction with the way in which so many girls seemed born only to be groomed for the marriage market, dissuaded from taking independent action by domineering adults who rendered them virtual prisoners in their own families. Frederica's story is, in some ways, a comical revisiting of the great epistolary novels of Samuel Richardson, but it also hints that the parodic surface of Jane Austen's early fiction was beginning to reveal new psychological depths and a readiness to explore the predicaments of real people.

The sympathy for Frederica that increasingly undermines Lady Susan's domination of her novel is a good indication of Jane Austen's literary development. Despite her attraction to the comic potential of the older woman in fiction, Austen herself was only just entering her twenties, and her imagination was more easily engaged by the possibilities and difficulties facing those of her own age. From Lady Susan, she turned her attentions to new, younger characters in the creation of two novels that would eventually be revised and published as *Sense and Sensibility* and *Pride and Prejudice*. Unfortunately, the manuscripts of the works she composed in the 1790s have not been preserved, so we can only speculate on the shape of 'Elinor and Marianne' and 'First Impressions'. It seems likely that both were at least partially epistolary in form, like *Lady Susan*, and that some of the letters eventually included in *Sense and Sensibility* and *Pride and Prejudice* had their origins in these earlier compositions. The focus of Jane Austen's later plots – on young women who suffer setbacks as a result of unreliable men, overbearing relations and social prejudices in their search for suitable partners – also has obvious foundations in the kind of life led by their author during the 1790s. More than this, however, can hardly be ascertained with any confidence.

What is clear, nevertheless, is that Jane's writing continued to command the respect of her family. An anecdote recounted many years later by her niece Anna describes an early family reading of the story that would become *Pride and Prejudice*; though it was deemed unsuitable for the ears of such a little girl, the recollection shows how much Anna's older relations enjoyed Aunt Jane's stories.[28] On Jane's nineteenth birthday, George Austen made a symbolic gesture of support by presenting her with a writing desk, but, by November 1797, he was ready to make the more public statement of sending 'First Impressions' to the leading London publishing house of Cadell & Davies. The offer of the manuscript was rejected by return of post, but any pangs of disappointment Jane may have felt were partially assuaged by the very idea of publication and by the parental faith embodied in George Austen's letter. It seemed only a matter of time before the talented young woman would become a published author.

BATH

1798–1804

'Well, here we are at Bath.'[29] When Jane Austen wrote to Cassandra in May 1799, at the beginning of a six-week visit, she was in good spirits, despite the dismal weather and her mother's ill health. As she had been to Bath before, her references to the fashionable venues and elegant streets – Sydney Gardens, Paragon, Queen's Parade – have the ease of familiarity as well as the frisson of expectation. In the weeks that followed, she became more optimistic about her mother's recovering strength and felt free to fill Cassandra in on the latest fashions in headwear and the most recent additions to their social circle. Eighteen months later, her attitude to Bath had changed completely. Instead of inhabiting her imagination as a dazzling white city, full of exciting strangers and outlandish outfits, offering the endless diversions of theatres, shops and public assemblies, it had become the destination of a dwindling family leaving its home for ever.

In 1800, George Austen announced his plan to retire from his duties as the parish priest at Steventon and to settle in Bath. Jane, as an unmarried daughter, would of course accompany her parents, and so, by the new year, she was planning her departure from the house where she had been born and had lived for twenty-five years. Family recollections have led to a general perception that the removal from beloved Hampshire to Bath was one of the great disasters of Jane Austen's life, but there is, as so often, very little direct evidence of her feelings on the matter. The letter she wrote in January 1801 is full of practical details about the relative living costs of different parts of Bath, but says little about her attachment to Steventon. Nevertheless, her confession to Cassandra – 'I get more & more reconciled to the idea of our removal' – suggests that the prospect of dislocation had been decidedly unwelcome.[30] Nor is this very surprising for an exceptionally sensitive woman whose entire life had centred on a country rectory surrounded by beautiful, rolling hills, thick with every kind of tree and criss-crossed by winding lanes with high, arching hedges. Bath had its own beauty. It was an exciting place to visit. But the idea of living there permanently was a very different matter.

Jane's explanation to Cassandra of her gradual reconciliation to the departure plan suggests a determination to find some positive angle on catastrophe: 'We have lived long enough in this Neighbourhood, the Basingstoke Balls are certainly on the decline, there is something in the bustle of going away, & the prospect of spending future summers by the Sea or in Wales is very delightful.'[31] The rapid accumulation of arguments makes each seem less persuasive than the last. Just as Elinor Dashwood would counsel her devastated younger sister to exert herself and conceal her distresses, Jane Austen appears to be rallying her own powers of self-possession in order to face an unavoidable fact. As her letter continues, she claims that leaving Steventon is no great sacrifice, and that she expects 'to inspire no tenderness, no interest in those we leave behind'. She is effectively voicing the lesson later inflicted on Anne Elliot at her most self-punishing, 'in the art of knowing our own nothingness beyond our own circle'.

Whatever the degree of distress induced by the departure from Hampshire, however, Bath did offer the possibility of a new life. Living in town might be noisy and unsettling, but it also meant a lot more people, some of whom might eventually emerge from the crowd as friends or even prospective husbands. As Jane Austen entered her late twenties, the pressure to marry was becoming more intense, so perhaps the balls in Bath would produce the right man at last? Any lingering thoughts about Tom Lefroy's admiration had taken on a very different complexion when news of his marriage to the Irish heiress Mary Paul had arrived in 1799. The other men who had figured in Austen's letters had found new girls to dance with, moved away or simply failed to ignite any real passion in her heart. Surely there was someone in Bath? And even if both she and Cassandra were destined to remain single, the complete change of scenery, daily routines and activities might well provide an immense boost to her writing.

When she first returned from the city in 1797, her imagination had, after all, been fired by a new sense of possibility. The reaction to a first encounter with Bath recorded in *Northanger Abbey* is drawn straight from recent experience: 'They arrived at Bath. Catherine was all eager delight; – her eyes were here, there, every where, as they approached its fine and striking environs, and afterwards drove through those streets which conducted them to the hotel. She was come to be happy, and she felt happy already.' Thoughts of Bath could generate intense happiness, as Jane Austen knew very well, but the pleasures of life in the city could also seem superficial and artificial, just like its residents. By the time she was revising *Northanger Abbey* for publication, during 1801 and 1802, her own ideas about Bath seem to have undergone very substantial alteration.

Although no manuscript has survived to offer clues about which passages belong to particular periods of composition, it seems likely that those conveying some of the less positive aspects of Bath belong to the process of revision rather than to the initial burst of creativity. In a conversation in the novel over the attractions of Bath, the newcomer's keen appetite for everything the city has to offer is carefully balanced against the more jaded perspective of the habitual visitor. Catherine's eager exclamations – 'Oh! Who can ever be tired of Bath?' – are carefully juxtaposed with Mr Tilney's more considered assessment: 'For six weeks I allow, Bath is pleasant enough; but beyond *that*, it is the most tiresome place in the world.' Neither view is complete, but together they may reflect Jane Austen's growing ability to invest traditional literary themes with the freshness of first-hand observation. In the same decade that William Blake created his *Songs of Innocence and of Experience*, Jane Austen was exploring the contrary states in relation to her own life and her literary development.

If, during her teens, Jane Austen had considered herself as being, like Catherine Morland, 'in training for a heroine', it was now perhaps dawning on her that she was more suited to take on the role of author. The narrative voice in *Northanger Abbey*, though infinitely sympathetic, is keen to emphasise the distance between the perspective of the storyteller and that of the main character. The rapid summary of Catherine Morland's life prior to the age of seventeen introduces readers to the affectionate irony of the all-seeing narrator, but offers no direct communication from the heroine herself. We do not hear Catherine's voice properly until halfway through the second chapter, when she whispers to Mrs Allen in the packed Upper Rooms: 'How uncomfortable it is not to have a single acquaintance here.' The difference between the heroine's own words and the highly sophisticated sentences that have prepared the reader for her debut is only too apparent and, while the novel steadily allows for increasing focus on Catherine's interior drama, its interest is sustained throughout by the narrator's self-consciously skilful commentary.

The joke about Catherine's status as a heroine is a natural development from the parodic character of Jane Austen's early writings. Her teenage compositions reveal a fascination with literary convention that emerges further in *Northanger Abbey*. The novel is much more substantial than early pieces such as 'The Beautiful Cassandra' or 'Henry and Eliza', with the exploration of literary matters integrated into a narrative that offers the additional satisfactions of convincing settings, astute observation, imaginative involvement with the characters and a proper plot. Its author had learned much about the development of different characters and the ways in which contrasting ideas could be conveyed through their letters when she wrote *Lady Susan*, but these discoveries were only the fore-runners of what she achieved in *Northanger Abbey*. One of the most obvious differences between the two works is form. As Mrs Morland says goodbye to her daughter at the beginning of *Northanger Abbey*, the narrator observes: 'It is remarkable . . . that she neither insisted on Catherine's writing by every post, nor exacted her promise of transmitting the character of every new acquaintance, nor a detail of every interesting conversation that Bath might produce.' In effect, Jane Austen was despatching both her heroine on her adventures and the epistolary novel to the honourable shades of literary history. Once she had abandoned the letter form favoured by Samuel Richardson and Frances Burney for their highly influential novels about the social challenges facing young women in the eighteenth century, Jane Austen was free to develop her own, independent narrative voice. Though she did not realise it at the time, she was also pioneering an entirely new kind of English fiction.

Jane Austen could not have predicted the future of the English novel when she worked on *Northanger Abbey*, but she was certainly very conscious of the possibilities of her chosen form. She also knew that not everyone was as enlightened. Before the family moved from Steventon, a circulating library had opened in the village, making it possible for local people to borrow books and thereby greatly increase their scope for reading. When the proprietor, Mrs Martin, asked the Austens to subscribe in December 1798, she assured them that her library would stock not just novels, but all kinds of literature – an overture that produced some amusement at the rectory: 'She might have spared this pretension to *our* family, who are great Novel-readers & not ashamed of being so.'[32] Nevertheless, they recognised that Mrs Martin's reassurances were probably necessary 'to the self-consequence of half of her Subscribers'. Today, the genre is so well established that it is hard to imagine a time when people were embarrassed to admit to being 'Novel-readers', but during Jane Austen's lifetime, novels were widely regarded as somewhat frivolous and even downright dangerous. For girls especially, reading fiction was often considered risky and generally undesirable. It was not every clergyman who would choose the latest Gothic fiction for his holiday reading, but Jane Austen describes her father engrossed in *The Midnight Bell* at the Bull and George in Dartford, on their way home from Kent in October 1798.[33] More unusual still was George Austen's readiness to share such books with his unmarried daughters.

When Jane Austen depicted Catherine Morland being introduced to the newest 'Horrid Novels' by Isabella Thorpe, she was playing on contemporary fears about the harmful influence of fiction – but, with a characteristic refusal to submit to prevailing assumptions, she used the scene as an opportunity to defend her favourite literary form. In answer to the dismissive attitude so common among her contemporaries – 'Oh! It is only a novel!' – the narrator of *Northanger Abbey* famously retorts that it is 'only some work in which the greatest powers of the mind are displayed, in which the most thorough knowledge of human nature, the happiest delineation of its varieties, the liveliest effusions of wit and humour are conveyed to the world in the best chosen language'. As she worked on her own novel, Jane Austen was beginning to recognise just what a task she was undertaking.

The celebration of fiction in *Northanger Abbey* extends well beyond the startling defence in chapter five. John Thorpe's failure to get through more than the first volume of Frances Burney's new novel is an indication of his other character deficiencies, while Henry Tilney's detailed knowledge of Mrs Radcliffe's work is one of his many charms. Although Catherine herself is led into excruciating misunderstandings by her undisciplined, Gothic-fuelled imagination, her unaffected pleasure in books, as in everything else, delights all those she meets, especially her own readers. As Jane Austen presented her heroine interpreting life according to the books she enjoyed, she was exploring the complexities of her own art and her responsibilities as a writer. When Catherine exclaims at Northanger, 'Oh! Mr Tilney, how frightful! – This is just like a book!', she demonstrates her author's sophisticated understanding of the dimensions of fiction. Not only does the narrator prompt us to consider what we are doing when we read a novel, so do the characters. Catherine Morland's propensity to see herself in a fictional world is, after all, understandable enough, given that she is a character in a novel.

In her early writing, Jane Austen had moved happily between the recognisable world of Hampshire and the realms of her own reading, revelling in the comedy that could be extracted from sudden jumps from one to the other. Now she explored an altogether more subtle kind of fiction, in which the literary and the real cohabited far more harmoniously. Crucial to the success of her new novel was its more realistic representation of settings, conversations and action. Familiarity with Bath enabled Jane Austen to create a fictional world that instantly rings true. Unlike the Scottish or Welsh references in 'Lesley Castle' or 'Love and Freindship', the city in *Northanger Abbey* is a real place, conjured up by the names of streets and buildings that occur naturally in the course of the narrative. 'They were soon settled in comfortable lodgings in Pulteney Street' has a matter-of-fact quality that enables readers to enter into the world of the novel, whether or not they have any first-hand knowledge of Bath. The description of Catherine's journey in John Thorpe's carriage through Laura Place and into Argyle Buildings is so convincing that the heroine's distress seems only too real, just as her subsequent enjoyment of the ball is enhanced for readers by its taking place in the Octagon Room. No detailed description of the architecture of Bath is given, but the way in which both characters and narrator refer to the various venues, just as readers might describe things to a local friend, is far more effective than an elaboration of sash windows, Sheraton tables and chandeliers.

Bath offered more than a rich landscape for Jane Austen's characters. Apart from her early educational experiences, she had spent much of her life in the company of her own extended family and the neighbours who lived in the parsonages and manor houses round about. She knew the servants at home and the labourers who worked in the nearby fields. She went to the shops in Overton and the balls in Basingstoke. She had stayed in Kent when visiting Edward's family and had been to London to see Henry. Beyond this, however, Jane Austen's experience of human life was not very extensive, and so Bath's appeal to people of all ages and varied backgrounds greatly increased her knowledge of the world. Mrs Allen's obsession with muslins, for example, is beautifully observed and, though reminiscent in some ways of Charlotte Luttrell's preoccupation with food in 'Lesley Castle', conveys all the atmosphere of 1790s Bath. Nor were Jane Austen's horizons broadened by only the enormous range of individuals who came and went for medical or social reasons. She was able to experience life in town and to develop ways of recreating a smart, urban environment in her fiction. Catherine Morland's first excursion vividly evokes the alarm that may be felt by a girl from the country who finds herself overwhelmed by a mass of strangers in a confined space. Once adjusted to Bath, however, Catherine is able to navigate the streets with ease, while her creator uses the skilfully evoked sense of endless movement to introduce new characters and chance encounters unexpectedly, though not improbably.

If Bath provided a stimulating environment for Jane Austen's active imagination, it also offered daily reminders of what might result from determined efforts to shape language, wit and human interest into an engaging narrative. At Steventon, the opening of a circulating library was a major event. Bath, on the other hand, was so well endowed with bookshops and libraries that the Austen family was able to keep up with the latest publications far more easily. To be surrounded by new books, and, equally importantly, by people who bought new books, was likely as crucial to Jane Austen's development as the fresh material that furnished her inner world. Although 'First Impressions' had been rejected out of hand, it seemed worth having another attempt at convincing a publisher that her work was worthy of attention. Crosby & Co. had outlets in the Bath book trade and published a considerable range of titles, including domestic and Gothic novels. The firm was doing well, made efforts to market its books effectively and welcomed 'eye-catching' scripts.[34] Henry was now established as a banker in London and, with the help of one of his new contacts, William Seymour, Jane Austen's novel found its way into the offices of Crosby & Co. early in 1803. To the author's very great delight, it was accepted.

At this stage of its development, the novel eventually published as *Northanger Abbey* was called 'Susan', a title that made its first public appearance among the lists of new books being advertised by Crosby within months of acceptance. Such rapid literary success must have done much to ease any residual sadness over departure from rural Hampshire and help reconcile Jane Austen to her new urban lifestyle. Not yet thirty, Jane's talents were being recognised beyond the warm, but inevitably partial, gaze of her immediate family. The ability that had always been channelled into private entertainments was now to find a much larger audience. 'Susan' was about to make her entrance into society, and she was ready to be jostled and admired by a crowd of unknown readers.

The novel, however, did not appear. Despite his agreement to publish, and the fee of £10 sent by Crosby in return for the manuscript, his firm never printed 'Susan'. Nor did he give any reason for his decision to withhold publication. Gradually, the months of waiting for news of the book turned into years. The heady joy of acceptance became the hard fact of rejection. For a single woman approaching her thirtieth birthday in the early nineteenth century, the feeling of being unwanted was beginning to close in on Jane Austen from various directions.

FROM HOME TO HOME

1804–9

'But you know we must marry.'[35] It is not difficult to discern some of Jane Austen's own preoccupations behind the dialogue she began to draft after her first novel had been sent off to the publishers. She abandoned 'The Watsons' after only forty pages, but what survives of her story reveals much about a writer whose life seemed oddly suspended between hope and disappointment. The fragment opens with Emma Watson returning to her immediate family after growing up in the happy home of an aunt who has just remarried and gone to join her new husband in Ireland. On the journey into Surrey, Emma is accompanied by her elder sister Elizabeth, who seizes the opportunity to recount the sorry tale of her broken romance, while insisting that Emma must, nevertheless, find herself a husband. The reason the Watson sisters are faced with no alternative to early marriage is economic: 'Father cannot provide for us, & it is very bad to grow old & be poor & laughed at.' Emma is shocked by her sister's words, and, reluctant to concur, insists: 'Poverty is a great Evil, but to a woman of Education & feeling it ought not, it cannot be the greatest . . . I would rather be Teacher at a school (and I can think of nothing worse) than marry a Man I did not like.' Although the satiric touch about teaching is reminiscent of the early writings, the tone of the conversation is altogether more serious, suggesting that its subject could not be kept entirely under comic control. The painful debate between two far-from-wealthy sisters about their possible futures was only too close to Jane Austen's own experience.

Emma Watson's resistance to the idea of pursuing a husband 'merely for the sake of situation' conveys a degree of anger at the predicament of women whose adult lives depended wholly on their ability to attract a sufficiently well-heeled man. Nor is her objection countered by her sister's wishful thinking: 'I think I could like any good humoured Man with a comfortable Income.' The difference of opinion points to Jane Austen's views on the matter, which would be spelt out with unequivocal clarity ten years later, in November 1814, when she counselled her niece Fanny Knight against any thought of marriage if she found herself still harbouring doubts about her feelings towards it: 'Anything is to be preferred or endured rather than marrying without Affection.' Despite the pressures so graphically portrayed in 'The Watsons', in which the need to secure a future home and husband turns Emma's sisters into desperate rivals, Jane Austen seems to have believed firmly that no one should marry without love. She had no illusions, however, about the difficulties facing those unlucky enough to be forced into the pursuit of love and failing to find it. This story, which she began after completing *Northanger Abbey*, addressed a problem she would revisit imaginatively throughout her life.

Jane Austen was a single woman living in a rented house with her sister and parents when she wrote 'The Watsons', but she could have been a wife and mistress of a country mansion in Hampshire. Two years earlier, in 1802, she had accepted a proposal of marriage from Harris Bigg-Wither, younger brother of her close friends Catherine and Alethea Bigg. She had been staying with the Bigg sisters at Manydown Park, on the way back from seeing Edward in Kent, when Harris, whom she had known since childhood, took the opportunity to ask Jane to marry him. She said 'yes' at once, but, by the very next morning, had changed her mind. Why? The most likely explanation is that she spent a very restless night agonising over her decision, before coming to the conclusion that she was not in love with Harris and was never likely to be. No amount of fondness for him, or for his sisters, could compensate for the absence of real, passionate love. He might be a good companion, he might inherit a wonderful estate only a few miles from Steventon, but she knew that it was better to remain a spinster, with a limited income and no permanent home, than to marry without the deepest emotional attachment. Her later advice to Fanny Knight was founded on personal conviction.

In 1802, Jane Austen was probably still hoping to fall in love with someone who might turn out to be her future husband. Even if Marianne Dashwood considered a woman of twenty-seven to be well past the age at which she might hope to inspire affection in a man, Jane Austen knew that plenty of people found romantic fulfilment beyond their early twenties. Eliza had not married Henry until 1797, when she was thirty-six. Whether Jane Austen suffered from the kind of feelings attributed to Elizabeth in 'The Watsons' ('A heart wounded like yours can have little inclination for Matrimony') is not known. Her early flirtation with Tom Lefroy has attracted a great deal of attention in recent years, inspiring a book, a film and an enormous amount of speculation.[36] The evidence relating to her emotional life, however, is frustratingly sparse. As so often, the few known facts are interesting enough to generate plenty of lively, imaginative interpretations, but are insufficient for establishing a full, authoritative account of crucial moments in her life. It seems just as possible that Jane Austen was in love with someone whose name has never been identified. Or she may have had a sequence of secret passions, the details of which were wisely kept from her extended family and would hardly have survived in her letters.

Little is known about the acquaintances, new friends or eligible bachelors whom Jane may have met during the years after the family moved from Hampshire. Though based in Bath, the Austens had holidays in Devonshire, Dorset and Sussex, admiring the scenery, swimming in the sea and, inevitably, attending parties in the fashionable seaside resorts. Long after Jane Austen's death, Cassandra admitted to their niece Caroline that her sister had fallen in love with a 'very charming man' ('I never heard Aunt Cass speak of anyone else with such admiration')[37] whom she had met on one of their summer visits to the coast. Apparently, they planned to continue seeing each other after the Austens went back to Bath, but the man, whose name remains a mystery, had died soon afterwards. If this experience belonged to the first summer trip to Sidmouth in 1801, it may have had a bearing on Jane Austen's initial confusion over Harris Bigg-Wither's proposal. It may also have altered her emotional life and general outlook for ever. But equally, it may not.

The impressions of Jane Austen that emerge from the early recollections suggest a person whose uneventful life remained largely untroubled by romantic entanglements, and whose devotion to her family and her writing was completely absorbing. Nevertheless, Henry Austen, James Edward Austen-Leigh and Caroline Austen all describe her as a very attractive woman. Her brother's account, written within months of his sister's death, describes her graceful way of moving, her fine complexion, her sweet voice and the delightfully expressive face that displayed so openly the 'cheerfulness, sensibility, and benevolence, which were her real characteristics'.[38] Her nephew's memories, though recorded half a century later, seem just as warm: 'In complexion she was a clear brunette with a rich colour; she had full round cheeks, with mouth and nose small and well formed, bright hazel eyes, and brown hair forming natural curls close round her face.'[39] Although he considered Aunt Jane less 'regularly handsome' than Aunt Cassandra, he was alert to her special attractions: '[H]er countenance had a peculiar charm of its own to the eyes of most beholders.' Such a woman would hardly have failed to attract admirers. Caroline, too, was clear that her aunt was 'established as a very pretty girl, in the opinion of most of her neighbours'.[40] Jane Austen clearly enjoyed parties and met plenty of men – perhaps she cared for none of them?

With no direct account of Jane Austen's private feelings, we can do nothing but speculate.

What is certain, however, is that when she represented the processes of love and courtship in her mature novels, she was able to capture the feelings of her heroines with unprecedented literary skill. It is hard to imagine a writer who had never been in love conveying Marianne Dashwood's sufferings with such care and sympathy, or depicting the overwhelming joy felt by Anne Elliot at the end of *Persuasion*. Throughout her mature fiction, the mysterious effects of love and desire are explored with an understanding that enables readers to respond to each heroine's emotional twists and turns as if she were a real person. Jane Austen's generous treatment of misconstrued attention or misplaced affection may result entirely from acute observation of those around her, but it seems unlikely. There may not be any definitive revelatory statement in a journal, or even in private letters, but Jane Austen left the evidence of her deep personal knowledge of the human heart in every one of the novels she published.

As for 'The Watsons', Austen may have abandoned it because it was addressing issues that potentially seemed too close to her own situation, or she may have been too distracted by a packed social diary and her frequent holidays and trips to visit family and friends. It is also possible that, as a serious writer, she knew her story just was not working. The non-publication of 'Susan' cannot have helped stimulate renewed creative energy, but there were plenty of other reasons for her to sink into low spirits. Mrs Austen's anxieties about her own health, which had often been something of a trial to her daughters ('she sometimes complains of an Asthma, a Dropsy, Water in her Chest & a Liver Disorder'), had become a real cause for concern since the onset of a more dangerous illness.[41] Although she recovered, the comic verse Jane wrote to celebrate paradoxically reveals the attack's seriousness: 'Says Death, "I've been trying these three weeks or more / To seize an old Madam here at Number Four."'[42] Death may have been disappointed on this occasion, but now that Mrs Austen was in her sixties, the possibility of things turning out differently next time was only too real.

Mrs Austen may have encouraged the family to laugh in the face of death, but there were situations in which even the most advanced sense of humour was powerless to help. Hastings's death in October 1801, at the age of fifteen, brought grief not only on account of the loss of the boy himself, but also for the thoughts it prompted about Jane's brother George, who had suffered from fits in his childhood so much like those that had afflicted Eliza's unlucky son. Three years later, Jane Austen's twenty-ninth birthday was darkened by the news that Mrs Lefroy had been killed suddenly when her horse had bolted during a routine shopping expedition to Overton. The extraordinary accident brought back painful memories of Jane Cooper's early death in a crashed carriage in 1798. But the worst was still to come. Within a month of Mrs Lefroy's fall, Jane Austen's father was dead.

Jane wrote at once to tell her brother Frank, describing the suddenness of their father's decline into 'fever, violent tremulousness, & the greatest degree of Feebleness'.[43] For once, all her comic energy was suspended. The comfort offered to her brother, whose shock she so thoughtfully anticipated, gives a rare insight into Jane Austen's own ultimate source of strength and consolation: her faith in her father's intrinsic goodness and his 'constant preparation for another World'. During the harrowing hours of his illness, Jane had joined her sister and mother in fervent prayers for his release from suffering, and, in the aftermath, she was similarly sustained by her faith. Nevertheless, the magnitude of her loss, and its practical effects on those left behind, cast a very dark cloud over her early thirties.

The death of George Austen left his widow and daughters in difficult circumstances. They remained in Bath for about a year, in more modest accommodation in Gay Street, before moving to Southampton, where Frank had set up home after his marriage to Mary Gibson in June 1806. When Frank went away to sea again the following year, his mother and sisters moved in, staying for the next two years. Although Jane had always been very conscious of Frank's naval career, living with his wife and helping care for their baby brought home the daily dangers of life at sea and the enormous relief of the captain's shore leave.

The years in Southampton, with Portsmouth nearby, gave Jane Austen her first experience of life in a major port, full of news about British engagements overseas and the progress of the war. She saw first-hand the great warships packed with men and cannon, the trading vessels and passenger boats, and the huge variety of people who filled the quayside. Southampton had its share of elegant buildings and balls, but the sense of purpose that galvanised so much activity at the harbour in Portsmouth offered a striking contrast to the leisurely and often ailing society of Bath. The final words of Jane Austen's last complete novel celebrate the domestic virtues and national importance of the British navy. Just as her earliest writings were meant as presents for her family, so too would she eventually use her published works to pay tribute to those whose support had meant so much to her, and whose merits she held in such high esteem.

If Frank had rescued his mother and sisters from the insecurities of temporary lodging by welcoming them into his growing household, it was Edward who eventually gave them a home of their own. His own life was shattered in 1808 by the sudden death of his wife Elizabeth a few days after giving birth. Cassandra was staying with the family at Godmersham when the devastating blow struck, leaving Edward inconsolable and his eleven children without a mother. While Cassandra tried to comfort Fanny and her little brothers and sisters, the two eldest boys, who were at school in Winchester, went to stay with Aunt Jane in Southampton. A letter to Cassandra written on 24 October describes Jane's efforts to divert their nephews with 'spillikins, paper ships, riddles, conundrums, and cards', but also makes reference to their own 'plans'. By October 1808, Mrs Austen and her daughters were being given the choice of moving to one of the smaller houses on Edward's estates in either Kent or Hampshire. They plumped for the latter, at Chawton, a few miles from Steventon, and, over the next few months, the plans turned into serious preparations.

The prospect of the move prompted Jane Austen to take positive action. After years of wondering what had happened to 'Susan', she decided to write to Crosby on 5 April 1809 asking whether they had lost the manuscript, signing her letter 'MAD' ('Mrs Ashton Dennis, Post Office, Southampton'). Her offer to replace it with another copy was answered curtly by Richard Crosby, who informed her that his firm was under no obligation to publish the novel, but it would take proceedings against any other publisher who did so. If she wanted to recover ownership of her work, she would need to reimburse Crosby the £10 originally paid for 'Susan'. Although Jane Austen abandoned the matter for the time being, her decision to get to grips with a situation that had been in unsatisfactory suspension for six years suggests a renewed sense of determination and a reviving optimism about her writing. Once safely installed at Chawton, if not with a room of her own, then at least with some space to write, Jane Austen began work on another novel. 'Susan' was imprisoned in a publisher's vault in London and Emma Watson had been abandoned, but there were other stories that Jane had drafted more than ten years before. 'Elinor and Marianne' came out of the cupboard and started to take on a new life, just as their author was doing.

Whatever Jane Austen had imagined for the two sisters in the middle of the 1790s could now be developed with far greater depth thanks to her experiences over the intervening years. Her new novel provided an opportunity to deal with the painful questions of parental death and expulsion from the family home and, although so many details concerning the Dashwood family were quite different from her own, the circumstances that now propelled the plot were things that Jane Austen knew about from direct exposure. Her fictional account of

Mrs Dashwood and her daughters being offered a cottage on the estate of a wealthy relative has an obvious connection to personal events. The brief description of the Dashwoods' new home in Devonshire as being a 'comfortable and compact' house, though 'defective' as a cottage, would have fitted Chawton Cottage, with its square-brick frontage, equally accurately.

The glimpse of the daughters 'endeavouring, by placing around them their books and other possessions, to form themselves a home' also allows an insight into Jane Austen's idea of what was most important in making unfamiliar surroundings feel homely. She had had plenty of experience placing books and other possessions into new rooms over the preceding eight years, but settling into Chawton Cottage carried an air of permanence. After the restless years in Bath and Southampton, with the numerous journeys to other towns and other people's houses, the Austen sisters had come to a halt in a small country village, not very far from the one in which they had grown up. It was a new stage of life, but it was also a return to something deeply familiar. Just as William Wordsworth was finding the rediscovery of his childhood home in the Lake District enormously reinvigorating, so too did Jane Austen's return to Hampshire provide the stimulus for the extraordinary creative outpouring of the next eight years.

SENSE AND SENSIBILITY AND PRIDE AND PREJUDICE

---◆•)◆(•◆---

1809–13

The first conversation between Elinor Dashwood and Colonel Brandon in *Sense and Sensibility* explores the benefits and disadvantages of gradual maturity. Jane Austen had already begun to use fictional dialogue as a way of presenting opposing views on important issues in both *Northanger Abbey* and 'The Watsons', and now she developed this technique in the novel she began to revise soon after her arrival in Chawton. When Elinor expresses her hopes that 'a few years' will modify her younger sister's romantic notions and 'settle her opinions on the reasonable basis of common sense and observation', Colonel Brandon replies, with surprising warmth, 'No, no, do not desire it, – for when the romantic refinements of a young mind are obliged to give way, how frequently are they succeeded by such opinions as are but too common, and too dangerous!' The exchange is reminiscent of Henry Tilney's admiration of Catherine Morland's innocent enthusiasm for the pleasures of Bath, but, in *Sense and Sensibility*, it is complicated by the focus on Marianne Dashwood, and the relative ages of Elinor and Colonel Brandon. Instead of the case for experience and rationality being made by the middle-aged, well-travelled military man, it is being argued by a young woman only two years older than the girl whose opinions she so confidently regards as being among the childish things that must be put away. The scene reveals not only Jane Austen's maturing style, but also her awareness that growing older can bring perils of its own. Elinor Dashwood might believe, from the advanced age of nineteen, that additional years inevitably beget good sense, but Colonel Brandon is able to voice the possibility that age might do nothing more than induce the jaded or commonplace.

For a creative writer, the thought that the idealistic or imaginative must inevitably be crushed by the rational and known was not necessarily something to celebrate. Even less welcome was the notion that the bright gleam of originality invariably faded into the light of common day. As Jane Austen reread the work she had first conceived fourteen years earlier, she was confronted with hard questions about whether the intervening period had brought the advantages anticipated by Elinor or the limitations observed by Colonel Brandon. If her novel was to succeed, she needed to find a way of retaining its early energy while restraining its excesses. As her writing developed, Jane Austen recognised that there were different ways of creating original works of art and that the skills acquired from experience and experimentation were ultimately as important as the initial sparks of inspiration. In *Sense and Sensibility*, however, the different elements that fuse with such powerful results in her mature fiction are seen as conflicting tendencies. Was imagination invariably at odds with reason? Impulsiveness with restraint? Sense with sensibility? The pain sustained by both the heroines, and by so many others in the novel, is indicative of the seriousness of a problem that was both artistic and moral. Jane Austen resolutely tackled the inherent difficulties of revising old work that somehow embodies a younger self, and, in the next work she prepared for publication, the mood is very much lighter and less troubled.

Although Jane Austen's early versions of the novel that became *Sense and Sensibility* have not survived, it is not difficult to see its connections with the unpublished works that were preserved. If it began life as an epistolary novel in 1795, then it probably had something in common with 'Love and Freindship', 'Lesley Castle' and *Lady Susan*.

Marianne's farewell to Norland, her views on matrimony and the weather, her accident, rescue, romance, broken heart and near-fatal illness – these might all have been conceived initially as a parody of contemporary sentimental fiction, like so many of Jane Austen's other pieces. When Laura and Sophia sigh and faint alternately on the sofa in 'Love and Freindship', it is designed to make fun of the literature of sensibility, with its swooning heroines and tearful heroes. In *Lady Susan*, Jane Austen took a different approach to the topic by creating a protagonist who seemed to lack any capacity for sympathy at all, but recognised the ways in which her more sensitive acquaintances could be manipulated. The largely realistic language and excessive selfishness of the central character, however, were paving the way towards a more subtle kind of humour, in which feeling might be allowed a place. As Jane Austen turned from *Lady Susan* to 'Elinor and Marianne', her new epistolary experiment probably attempted not only a more realistic style of correspondence than that of 'Love and Freindship', but also a more sympathetic representation of her young heroines' emotions.

Whether 'Elinor and Marianne' consisted entirely of the correspondence between sisters is not known, but it is easy to see how, in a first draft, Lucy Steele might have been represented largely through her own inelegant prose,

Marianne's romance with Willoughby might have flourished and been cut off through secret notes, or Colonel Brandon's past might have been revealed in a long letter. When Jane Austen initially revised 'Elinor and Marianne' in 1797–8, she may have introduced the distinctive narration also adopted for *Northanger Abbey*, transforming most of the fictional letters into conversations. That she modified Marianne Dashwood's expressions of sensibility at that stage, however, seems unlikely. Since *Northanger Abbey* includes self-conscious parody of Gothic novels, it is probable that the earlier alterations to 'Elinor and Marianne' would have been made to the narrative style and plot, but not to the spoof sensibility. By 1809, however, Jane Austen had begun to find the agonies of disappointed love less comical, or at least more worthy of serious consideration.

Although the novel has often been read as a critique of the contemporary 'cult of sensibility', it would be a mistake to assume that Jane Austen herself was unsympathetic to Marianne Dashwood. Since the books most admired by Marianne were also favourites of Jane Austen's, her creator would certainly have scored highly on Marianne's litmus test for sensibility. Jane Austen's letters, however, especially those written at excruciating moments, such as Elizabeth Austen's sudden death, suggest that she was also capable of exerting herself and concealing strong feelings in order to spare those of others – just as Elinor Dashwood does. When her brother James read *Sense and Sensibility*, he saw at once that both the Dashwood girls were based on his sister, the author:

On such subjects no Wonder that she shou'd write well,
In whom so united those qualities dwell;
Where 'dear Sensibility', Sterne's darling Maid,
With Sense so attemper'd is finely pourtray'd.
Fair Elinor's Self in that Mind is exprest,
And the Feelings of Marianne live in that Breast.[44]

The creation of an omniscient narrator meant, however, that Jane Austen's own personality could wear a number of different masks in her fiction; though both the Dashwood sisters may be self-portraits, they also work as independent creations and convincingly individual characters. The obvious contrast between them may derive from Jane Austen's own complicated internal divisions, but it also serves as a means of exploring ideas from different angles and revealing underlying unities in the face of more serious opposition.

Though Elinor quickly emerges as a figure of self-control and a foil for Marianne's more outspoken attitudes, both sisters are characterised by their sensitivity. The ridicule of sensibility that many readers have perceived in the novel is rapidly modified by much stronger criticism of those characters who lack any feeling for others: Marianne's passion for dead leaves has its comical aspect, but is still vastly preferable to the savage behaviour of Fanny Dashwood. If the revised novel retains some of the early jokes about contemporary literary trends, it is sustained by serious concerns about the conventions governing a society that prided itself on politeness. Despite the humorous surface, there is an underlying current of anger running through the scenes in which the open feelings of a healthy, seventeen-year-old girl are condemned as rude or unacceptable. Jane Austen's frustration over the suffering of young women at the hands of their friends and relations is nowhere more apparent than in *Sense and Sensibility*, even though the novel carries an overt warning against unguarded emotional confessions. Elinor's inclination to conceal the truth may prove to be wise counsel, but only because the Dashwood sisters are surrounded by self-seeking or insensitive characters who abuse their trust.

Rather than endorse the social codes that prove so stifling to Marianne's spirit, the novel criticises the hypocrisy of a society that seems civilised but offers little support to its more vulnerable members. Its sense of the injustices evident in everyday life and the way in which material success is not always enjoyed by the most deserving is apparent at once. After the death of Mr Dashwood, his daughters are ousted from their home by the unholy alliance of English inheritance law and their sister-in-law. The conversation may turn to gifts of china, but the actions being taken are brutal. The predicament of Mrs Dashwood and her three daughters makes an obvious comment on the dependency of wives, but this is itself qualified by the triumphant conquest of Norland that Fanny Dashwood accomplished through her own marriage. Jane Austen had developed a form in which her own experience could deepen her fiction because it was also tempered by rich knowledge of human society, drawn from years of careful observation. She knew very well that one family's misfortune often proved to be the making of another's prosperity, and that those on the way down were not necessarily spared further distress. Unlike so many of her contemporaries, however, she avoided a conventional presentation of suffering innocence, knowing that her story would carry greater conviction if the characters and their fortunes were more mixed, their afflictions closer to the real-life experiences of her readers.

Realistic portrayal of the problems confronting so many people also allowed for a kind of social comment that was profoundly felt, but free of the polemical tone that had seized so many novels in the revolutionary decade of the 1790s. The pressure to marry that made the start of

'The Watsons' so uncomfortable is again evident in the Dashwoods' enforced removal to Devonshire, and the embarrassing raillery to which they are then subjected at Barton Park. But it is countered by the devastating portrait of the Middletons, who fill their house with guests to dilute each other, or of Mr Palmer, who has been 'soured by finding, like many others of his sex, that through some unaccountable bias in favour of beauty, he was the husband of a very silly woman'. Marriage might be the cup awarded by contemporary society to successful young women, but Jane Austen was well aware that it sometimes proved, if not poisonous, then decidedly blighting. While some female characters in the novel gain great advantage from their marriages, others suffer years of dullness and even misery. As so often in her fiction, Jane Austen paints a society in which fortune seems fickle and human beings cope in different ways with the difficulties they suddenly find themselves facing. The problems are pervasive, but the means of tackling them are individual.

Despite its clear-sighted condemnation of individual shortcomings and prevailing social assumptions, however, the outlook of *Sense and Sensibility* is far from bleak. Some of those apparently introduced to try the patience of the heroines turn out to be their truest friends. Marianne's almost allergic reaction to Mrs Jennings, for example, is eventually shown to have been mistaken, while her quick judgement of Colonel Brandon and his flannel waistcoat is inverted completely. The negative portrayal of so many marriages is largely forgotten in the happiness that radiates from Elinor's eventual union, which brings the potential tragedy of the novel to a traditional comedic conclusion. Her new narrative style, with its sympathetic focus on the Dashwood sisters and their varying responses to the world, enabled Jane Austen to qualify points without sacrificing consistency.

Though far more restrained in tone than her anarchic early writings, *Sense and Sensibility* demonstrates a new kind of narrative freedom. In *Northanger Abbey*, Jane Austen had shown her interest in developing more convincing characters and a plot that could fully engage the reader, but in *Sense and Sensibility* she allowed real emotion into her narrative. Readers are encouraged not only to see the funny side of Austen's young heroines, but also to mind very much about what they are forced to endure: the suspense of the novel depends on imaginative involvement with their lives. The handling of Marianne's disappointment at discovering that the gentleman approaching on horseback is Edward Ferrars has a psychological acuteness that lifts the novel above mockery *and* sentimentality. Though still full of unresolved tensions, *Sense and Sensibility* is marked by Jane Austen's peculiar genius, and makes an astonishing debut publication for a novelist.

Once Jane Austen had relaxed the parodic grip on her storytelling, she had no difficulty in finding a publisher. Contemporary conventions initially prevented her from conducting her own business transactions, but, fortunately, Henry Austen was more than happy to act as her literary agent. He offered *Sense and Sensibility* to the London-based firm of Thomas Egerton, which accepted it at once. Although the agreement meant that Jane Austen would bear the production costs if the novel failed to sell, the risk turned out to have been well worth taking. *Sense and Sensibility* was published in October 1811, and immediately began to attract attention. Critical notices appeared in the press and, within three months of publication, the novel was being enjoyed in court, with no less prominent a reader than Princess Charlotte confessing to be among its admirers. Within two years, the first edition had completely sold out, making Jane Austen the handsome profit of £140. By then, she was hard at work on *Mansfield Park*, but, in the meantime, Thomas Egerton had shrewdly offered to buy the copyright of the novel that had begun to occupy her as soon as *Sense and Sensibility* was finished – *Pride and Prejudice*.

The confidence that came with publication shines out of every chapter of Jane Austen's next novel. She herself described *Pride and Prejudice* as 'too light & bright & sparkling', but this was hardly a confession of artistic failure.[45] Once *Sense and Sensibility* had been accepted and was making its way into print, Jane Austen had turned her newly developed skills towards the old family favourite, 'First Impressions'. Rejections might eventually be regretted more profoundly by those who had made them than by those who had been spurned, as Jane Austen's revisions made abundantly clear. Both Cadell and Crosby would come to rue their failure to spot the true value of the works once submitted to their firms by the author of *Sense and Sensibility*. In *Pride and Prejudice*, hasty judgements and prolonged repentance are treated with all the exuberant humour of one whose own undervalued brilliance has at last been recognised. When Elizabeth Bennet is slighted by Mr Darcy at the Meryton assembly, her response is cheerfully resilient: 'She told the story however with great spirit among her friends; for she had a lively, playful disposition, which delighted in any thing ridiculous.' Her author's temperament was similarly playful and, after years of silence and insecurity, she was now ready to turn painful experiences into funny stories, extending her circle to a vast audience of delighted admirers.

The extent of Jane Austen's revisions to 'First Impressions' is no more certain than that of the transformation of the earlier versions of *Northanger Abbey* and *Sense and Sensibility*. No manuscripts survive to make detailed comparison possible. Jane Austen admitted in a letter to Cassandra that she had 'lopt and cropt' the story, but there are also references to her 'writing', which suggests fresh composition. The atmosphere of the novel captures the mood of the earlier letters, when Jane was in her twenties and describing her triumphs and disappointments on the dance floor. This smacks of its original creation in 1797 and it seems likely that, as Jane Austen revised the story in 1811–12, she reread some of the letters preserved by her sister, incorporating memories prompted by the details. The balls in *Pride and Prejudice* may owe something to the Steventon Christmas ball of 1798, for example, at which Jane remembered 'Mr Calland, who appeared as usual with his hat in his hand, & stood every now and then behind Catherine & me to be talked to & abused for not dancing'.[46] If this suggests that Elizabeth Bennet is a portrait of the author's younger self, however, it is important to notice that, as the letter continues, we begin to hear more of Lydia: 'We teized him however into it at last; – I was very glad to see him after so long a separation, & he was rather the Genius & Flirt of the Evening.' Jane Austen not only had the draft of a novel, but also a stash of letters and personal experience to furnish her with the materials for her next book. Most important of all was the knowledge that it was the *next* book – that she was an author whose work mattered.

In *Sense and Sensibility*, Jane Austen seems to be exploring a series of conflicts that have to be resolved in secrecy, but in *Pride and Prejudice* everything opens up. Where Elinor's caution about revealing feelings is endorsed by the course of the narrative, Jane Bennet's proves almost disastrous. Mr Darcy's failure to expose Wickham's character means that Lydia and her family are unprepared for his predatory behaviour, while Darcy's own clumsiness in expressing emotion results in many pages of mortification. The openness of *Pride and Prejudice* is very different from that of *Sense and Sensibility*, for Elizabeth's outspoken wit offends only those characters whose outlook already seems inadequate. Unlike Marianne, who suffers public disapproval and personal anguish for her impulsiveness, Elizabeth behaves spontaneously and wins the immediate admiration of those who matter. Both heroines run, but where Marianne symbolically slips and falls, Elizabeth crosses 'field after field at a quick pace, jumping over stiles and springing over puddles'. Nothing deters her, and the novel celebrates the success of a woman whose refusal to be cowed or uncomfortably confined leads eventually to personal happiness. In *Sense and Sensibility*, everything seems very difficult, but *Pride and Prejudice* exults in its own sense of possibility.

Though so much lighter in tone than its predecessor, *Pride and Prejudice* is not without similar social concerns and sympathies. Again, the precarious situation of contemporary women is evident, but the iniquities of a system of male inheritance are now treated with comedy, by making it a subject 'on which Mrs Bennet was beyond the reach of reason'. Her husband's laconic recitation of the letter from his cousin Mr Collins ('who, when I am dead, may turn you all out of this house as soon as he pleases') shows that the Bennet daughters are no more secure than the Dashwoods, but it also reassures readers that, in such a good-humoured novel, nothing very distressing is likely to take place. Even when Charlotte Lucas accepts a husband for whom she can have little feeling, because, at twenty-seven, she needs a 'comfortable home', the potential misery is diffused by the force of Jane Austen's fine comic touches. When Elizabeth visits the married couple, the more painful aspect of her perceptive observation is balanced by the wit of its expression: 'When Mr Collins could be forgotten, there was really a great air of comfort throughout, and by Charlotte's evident enjoyment of it, Elizabeth supposed he must be often forgotten.' There is an additional joke, however, in the very idea that Charlotte's new husband could ever be forgotten.

Mr Collins, like Mrs Bennet and Lady Catherine de Bourgh, provides an exuberant kind of entertainment quite distinct from the quick wit of Elizabeth and her father, or from the embarrassing situational comedy of the Bennet family, or from the satirised speeches of Sir William Lucas and the Bingley sisters. The attitudes of these characters are exaggerated almost to the point of caricature, but the interaction with less extravagant creations keeps them within the realms of credibility, and thus crucial to the overall success of the narrative. The cast is vivid and varied, but no one is introduced purely to provide a comic interlude. *Pride and Prejudice* is controlled with great care, as character after character enters at just the right moment to fulfil their special role in the narrative design.

The witty, conversational tone of the novel's narrator keeps the story firmly grounded in the matter-of-fact, and Jane Austen was able to draw on the comedies she had seen performed first at home in Steventon and later in the professional theatres of Bath, London and Southampton. She had learned to love figures like Mrs Malaprop and Sir Lucius O'Trigger in her childhood, and now she had the confidence to create characters whose comic magnificence would surpass those of Sheridan by emerging so startlingly from the pages of a realistic novel. The kind of dialogue that propelled *The Rivals* or *The School for Scandal* could also be adapted for *Pride and Prejudice*, if only the characters' voices could be distinguished sufficiently. With scenes that depicted five sisters at home, the need to create lines that were both convincingly natural and instantly recognisable was paramount. Elizabeth commands attention by her lively conciseness ('Compliments always take *you* by surprise, and *me* never'), to which her elder sister provides the perfect foil. Lydia, as the youngest daughter, competes by using slang words ('Lord!') and mentioning the names of officers, while Kitty is reduced to coughing and exclamations. Mary, 'the only plain one in the family', has to rely on her determined accomplishments, and interrupts conversations with either a long quotation from a moral essay or an even longer concerto. Each daughter is easily identifiable through her speech and, in *Pride and Prejudice*, Jane Austen developed her skills in characterisation by adapting the techniques of the stage to her endlessly flexible pages.

The boldness of her new novel was not confined to its artistic innovations, however. In addition to the delightfully irreverent heroine, whose general attitudes provide such a refreshing contrast to the kinds of models promoted in the contemporary educational manuals for girls, Jane Austen presented her readers with a story that involves abductions and extramarital sex. The worst fears of eighteenth-century moralists are realised in the behaviour of George Wickham, but, far from following the literary convention of condemning either the rake or his victims, Jane Austen rescued both Georgiana and Lydia from social disgrace and punished Wickham with nothing harsher than a silly wife.

Unlike Richardson's novels, the focus of *Pride and Prejudice* is not on the seduction of the younger girls, but rather on the embarrassment of their elder sisters. As with the comic containment of Mr Bennet's threatened demise, there is never any real sense that Lydia's elopement will lead to her destruction, but the distressing effects of her rash actions on the rest of the family are still examined with great sensitivity. Despite its effervescent humour, *Pride and Prejudice* is just as concerned with the feelings of its heroines, whose contrasting responses to their changing circumstances lie at the heart of the novel. Readers may laugh at the novel's dazzling line-up of comic turns or marvel at the brilliant observations of human interactions; they may admire the skilful construction of the plot or the beautifully turned sentences from which it is made; they may be provoked into deeper consideration of the flaws in English society or the evasive wartime setting – but everyone who enjoys *Pride and Prejudice* will be compelled by the central narrative. Though Mrs Bennet's now-famous assumption that 'a single man in possession of a good fortune must be in want of a wife' is relentlessly mocked throughout, there can be few readers who remain immune to the intense satisfaction of the final union. *Pride and Prejudice* has many facets, but, like *Sense and Sensibility*, it is essentially a love story. Unlike its immediate predecessor, however, *Pride and Prejudice* is prepared to offer the possibility of unreserved happiness.

MANSFIELD PARK AND EMMA

1813–15

The intensity of Jane Austen's preoccupation with her writing cannot be overstated. Although her nephew's recollections conjure up a picture of the modest aunt quickly putting aside her writing at the sound of approaching visitors as if producing tea and conversation were every bit as important to her as creating such a scene on paper, her own letters tell a different story. A sisterly enquiry about the progress of *Sense and Sensibility* provoked an unusual metaphor: 'No indeed, I am never too busy to think of S&S. I can no more forget it than a mother forget her sucking child.'[47] It recurs two years later to express Jane's excitement over the arrival of *Pride and Prejudice*: 'I want to tell you that I have got my own darling Child from London.'[48] The comments jump out from the correspondence as rare revelations of genuine feeling, unmasked by irony, self-deprecation or comic absurdity. Jane Austen was referring to her novels as her children. By now, she was a single woman approaching forty, so the likelihood of having a baby of her own was remote. Instead of children, Jane Austen was producing books; and the affection with which she talks about the characters of *Pride and Prejudice* in letters to Cassandra demonstrates that the emotional satisfaction she derived from writing was profound.

Although Jane Austen never experienced motherhood, she maintained a deep interest in education and the ways in which children might be affected by their upbringing. Edward's large family provided an endless topic for Jane's own mother, while James and Frank's children, who lived much nearer Chawton Cottage, were frequent visitors. Jane's eldest nieces, Anna Austen and Fanny Knight (whose name had changed in 1812 when Edward inherited his estate), were now the same age as the Dashwood sisters and the Bennets, so she had plenty of opportunity to witness the trials of adolescence and early adulthood at first hand. As Jane Austen watched her nephews and nieces growing up, she was also reminded of her own childhood, alerted to the contrasts and the continuities between younger and older selves. Had she changed? Had Cassandra? Or James? Or any of her siblings? What made people grow into the adults they became? How important were their physical surroundings or material possessions? Were personalities fixed from birth or did the combined influence of education, family, place and income determine a child's character? Or was it the result of an individual's unique experiences?

These were questions that had already occupied many of the greatest minds of the past century and continued to attract vigorous debate. Jane Austen's approach was always primarily imaginative rather than purely philosophical, her mind moved by the human dimensions of a question. When she read essays, she responded passionately to their authors, even if the subject was as unpromising as Captain Pasley's *Essay on the Military Policy and Institutions of the British Empire* ('I am as much in love with the Author as I ever was with Clarkson or Buchanan,' she wrote on 24 January 1813). When she considered political or theoretical ideas, they rapidly changed into the conversations and behaviour of her imaginary creations. As a girl, her history lessons had provoked intense involvement with injured queens and indignation over detestable monsters. Now, her imagination was under tighter control, but the capacity to translate dry fact and argument into compelling human drama remained. The primary concern of her novels was the creation of believable human beings in a beautifully structured fictional world. By the time she wrote *Mansfield Park*, however, she knew that her acute observations of human behaviour might be conveyed in such a way that larger questions could also be addressed in her fiction.

In 1812, with the contract for *Pride and Prejudice* agreed, Jane Austen was bursting with ideas for her next novel. Rather than reach into her treasure trove of older writings to retrieve *Lady Susan* or 'The Watsons', she embarked on an entirely new story that would allow her to explore questions of education, family relationships and the different kinds of lives forced on individuals by their birth and background. She had not abandoned the imaginative stocks of her earlier years, but rather than revise stories written twenty years before, she now drew creatively on memories of Steventon or Southampton, revisiting in her mental landscape the English country houses of old friends and family. She was still interested in sisters, but now her attention turned from the necessity of marriage to its consequences, as she imagined the contrasting households of the three Miss Wards. Charlotte Lucas's wry observation that 'happiness in marriage was entirely a matter of chance' is tested in *Mansfield Park* through the cameo portraits of the three sisters and their relative successes: Maria's captivation of Sir Thomas Bertram; her elder sister's subsequent marriage to Reverend Norris; and the impulsive secret wedding of Frances and

Lieutenant Price, a low-ranking officer in an unelevated branch of the navy. Two married for love, but while one lives a life of easy luxury, the other is worn down by frequent pregnancies and the struggle of maintaining a large family on a low income. The economic and social divisions of contemporary society, which had furnished *Pride and Prejudice* with a rich seam of jokes about snobbery, upward mobility and the erotic charge of a good estate, were now providing the framework for a novel whose tone was far less 'light & bright & sparkling'. Frances Ward pays a heavy price for her unlucky infatuation: her married name is a constant reminder of her mistake.

Jane Austen was far too thoughtful a writer to be content with presenting any straightforward equation between material comfort and happiness. As the fast-paced, schematic opening chapter leads into the more slow-moving and capacious surroundings of Mansfield Park, initial judgements are qualified by the complexity of the narrative and its focus on the next generation. The transplantation of a child into an unfamiliar environment had always been a sensitive issue for the Austen family. Jane's decision to remove Fanny Price at 'just ten years old' from her home in Portsmouth drew on a cluster of painful, personal memories: Edward's adoption by the Knights; George's permanent exile; her departure for school and the experiences that followed. As she recreated the intense unhappiness of the displaced child, lost in the vast grandeur of her uncle's great house, however, Jane Austen was also breaking new narrative ground, shifting rapidly between profound sympathy for the vulnerable heroine and satirical comment on the unattractive figures who surround her. Fanny Price may not be able to defend herself, but the narrator is well equipped to demolish her oppressors with a caustic aside.

Despite the unsentimental attitude to Frances Ward's misguided romance, it quickly becomes apparent that the comfortable upbringing enjoyed by her elder sister's children has done nothing to ensure their personal well-being. One of the central ironies of the novel is that Mrs Price's apparently disastrous choice has nevertheless resulted in the birth of Fanny, William and Susan, who are all presented as far more admirable characters than their spoilt cousins. If Austen avoided equating wealth and goodness, however, neither was she endorsing Sir Thomas's final realisation of 'the advantages of early hardship and discipline, and the consciousness of being born to struggle and endure'. Sir Thomas's second son, Edmund, turned out well even without the advantages his father suddenly identifies as key to the integrity of the young Prices. It is evident from the closing chapters that the older generation have been just as much in need of a sound education as their children and that much of the unhappiness depicted in the novel has resulted from irresponsible parenting.

Henry Crawford has been 'ruined by early independence and bad domestic example', while Julia Bertram's marginal superiority to her sister has resulted from her being 'less the darling' of Mrs Norris, 'less flattered and less spoilt'.

Although *Mansfield Park* is clear about the unfortunate consequences of spoiling children, it also demonstrates that there are no easy answers to the question of what constitutes a good education or a good person. Despite the obvious sympathy for Fanny as a victim of bullying relations, she has not proven as universally appealing as Elizabeth Bennet, whom Jane Austen herself pronounced to be 'as delightful a creature as ever appeared in print'.[49] Many readers have balked at the seriousness of Fanny and Edmund, their embarrassment over naughty jokes or amateur dramatics, and the understated nature of their final declaration. Fanny's mounting horror at the noise levels in her own parents' home, her relief at returning to the tranquillity of Mansfield Park, despite its many flaws, and her disapproval of so many of the residents and their guests have not helped to endear her to readers already disappointed by her lack of wit and energy. In *Mansfield Park*, Jane Austen was marking out new territory as a novelist. She was no longer limited to her close family audience, who expected to be delighted, and could therefore experiment with a different kind of fiction. In her next novel, she would deliberately create a heroine whom 'no one but myself' would much like, but the idea of discomforting her readers was already well developed in *Mansfield Park*.⁵⁰

As a mature novelist, Jane Austen felt no need to use her work as a vehicle for submerged autobiography, even though she drew from the rich store of memories she had garnered over the years. The Bertram–Crawford theatricals gain conviction from her early experience of the rehearsals at Steventon, but these chapters fulfil many different roles in *Mansfield Park*. They develop the plot by introducing new characters and revealing different aspects of those already in place, while also offering a sophisticated exploration of the nature of art and the ways in which a play can become part of a novel. The major themes of class, education and personal choice are also highlighted as soon as Edmund expresses his reservations about fashionable private productions by 'a set of gentlemen and ladies who have all the disadvantages of education and decorum to struggle through'. Whatever Jane Austen's own memories, the theatricals constitute a beautifully crafted episode, intricately connected to numerous threads in the novel. In her skilled hands, the raw material of personal experience is transformed into fine art.

Similarly, references to William Price's promotion and the various ships in Portsmouth owe much to Frank and Charles Austen's naval careers, but this does not mean that the navy is included for the sake of family interest alone. William's wide experience of the world provides another comment on the disadvantages of gentlemen, most explicit when an eager account of his hazardous profession prompts Henry Crawford to a rare moment of self-knowledge: 'The glory of heroism, of usefulness, of exertion, of endurance, made his own habits of selfish indulgence appear in shameful contrast; and he wished he had been a William Price.' Jane Austen was paying a private tribute to her own brothers in her portrait of William, but she was also making more ambitious points about contemporary class structure, systems of inheritance and personal responsibilities to society. The careful contrasts between those in the navy and those born into wealth gradually make plain that *Mansfield Park*'s concern with economics is national as well as domestic. Jane Austen was too accomplished a novelist to allow family loyalties to cloud her acute observation of the ironies of contemporary society, however: the positive portrayal of Midshipman William Price is set against those of his rather less upstanding father and of the Crawfords' pleasure-loving uncle, the admiral.

Questions about the proper use of riches had attracted writers throughout the eighteenth century, but now took on a new urgency in relation to the French Revolution and the immediate Regency crisis. By 1813, when Jane Austen was writing *Mansfield Park*, the extravagance of the Prince Regent was legendary. Tales of his lavish parties and building projects startled his subjects, especially since many were struggling for survival by working very long hours in appalling conditions. There was even concern during the long war with France that, while the Prince Regent indulged in six-course banquets, the nation's food supply was actually running out, leaving the poor starving. At the same time, the recent campaign to abolish the slave trade had raised public awareness that part of Britain's prosperity had depended on the cruellest exploitation of human beings. Though patriotic loyalty was accentuated by Napoleon's alarming conquests abroad, doubts about the nation's domestic well-being were widespread.

Although Jane Austen's novels, with their carefully realised domestic settings, seem largely untroubled by the great issues of her day, it is evident from comments in her letters that she was extremely concerned about the human aspects of contemporary political questions. Her dislike of the Prince Regent, for example, was expressed most clearly in her sympathy for the Princess of Wales ('Poor Woman! I shall support her as long as I can, because she *is* a Woman, & because I hate her Husband'), while her keen interest in the abolition of the slave trade is evident in her 'love' of the campaigner Thomas Clarkson.[51] *Mansfield Park* avoids conversations about contemporary politics, but, in its imaginative exploration of the rights and wrongs of private economies, it addresses questions of intense public concern. When Fanny Price asks her uncle about the slave trade upon his return from Antigua, her question is answered with silence, even though her relations are happy to discuss the fashionable topics of landscape gardening, home improvements or the delivery of sermons. Jane Austen allowed nothing improbable, nothing contrived, into her new novel, but nevertheless developed ways of suggesting that the realistic details in her text were also signs of much broader concerns. Sir Thomas's 'recent losses on his West India Estate, in addition to his elder son's extravagance' were, after all, anxieties of which George III might have complained in his more lucid moments, and the discussions over whether alterations to an ancient inheritance should involve massive destruction or mere modification applied as much to the British constitution as to Mr Rushworth's house at Sotherton.

Mansfield Park is not a political novel in the sense that its purpose is polemical or its action allegorical, but, in the careful detail and thoughtful construction of contrasting characters, it demonstrates the ways in which a novel can offer numerous satisfactions. Like *Sense and Sensibility* and *Pride and Prejudice*, it has a strong plot, brilliant comic observation and sympathetic involvement with characters in realistic settings, but it also provided a new forum for testing contemporary ideas in action. The high ideals of the modern novel first set out in *Northanger Abbey* were rapidly being realised.

Jane Austen's interest in the economic basis of society was undoubtedly sharpened by her own circumstances. Unlike the Bertram daughters, she had not been born into a wealthy, landed family, even though many of her friends and relations had inherited estates. After her father's death, Jane Austen had spent years in rented houses and she remained dependent for a home on the charity of her brothers. The success of her novels gave her an income for the first time in her life and, with it, a renewed self-confidence and a different angle on the very idea of independence. In *Mansfield Park*, she had focused on the figure of the poor relation, but in her next novel she would explore similar questions of wealth, power, responsibility, education and the accidents of birth from the perspective of the wealthy instead. The very first line introduces Emma Woodhouse, 'handsome, clever and rich'. It is almost as though Fanny Price has been displaced by Maria Bertram.

Even before readers had arrived at chapter one, though, *Emma*'s distinction from the earlier novels was apparent from its new publisher – the fashionable firm of John Murray – and from the surprising dedication to 'His Royal Highness, the Prince Regent'. *Emma* was clearly receiving the best treatment because, like the heroine, it could not put up with any other. Despite the confidence exuded by her new novel, and despite the example set by Murray's most famous author, Lord Byron, Jane Austen did little to exploit her own chance to become a literary celebrity. *Emma* was dedicated to the Prince Regent not because Jane Austen wanted to flatter the future king, but because he had declared himself an admirer. All her novels had been published anonymously, but, by the time *Mansfield Park* appeared, her authorship was widely known. Henry, especially, found it difficult to keep quiet when he heard his sister's books being discussed, as Jane reported to Frank: 'Henry heard P.&P. warmly praised in Scotland, by Lady Robt. Kerr & another Lady; – & what does he do in the warmth of Brotherly vanity & Love, but immediately tell them who wrote it!'[52] She was clearly torn between dismay that the great secret, once out, would never be contained again, and delight in Henry's obvious pride in her success: 'A Thing once set going in that way – one knows how it spreads! – and he, dear Creature, has set it going so much more than once. I know it is all done from affection & partiality.' Since Henry had lost Eliza to cancer only a few months before, Jane was prepared to forgive him anything, but she was more grateful to Frank for his respect for her wishes. Public recognition was not an unmixed blessing, as she discovered when summoned to Carlton House by the Prince Regent's librarian. She could hardly refuse to dedicate her novel to the future king once he had decided to bestow royal patronage, but those closest to her smiled at the sight of the grand flourish, remembering her earlier, decidedly parodic dedications. No doubt the authoress enjoyed the irony of attracting royal patronage for a novel set more firmly than any of her others in a quiet corner of the kingdom.

Emma is a novel of rural retirement, in which London, Bath and Richmond are mentioned only as the distant destinations of characters disappearing from centre stage. Unlike the peripatetic heroines of her previous books, Emma remains at home and travels only a few miles in the entire course of the narrative. Of all Jane Austen's protagonists, however, Emma Woodhouse is the least retiring. *Mansfield Park* began by emphasising the range of characters contributing to the narrative, but *Emma* concentrates from the first on its heroine. Although she is a younger sister like Elizabeth Bennet or Marianne Dashwood, Emma dominates her novel in an entirely new way, with much of the narrative conveyed through her confident, if often mistaken, perception of those around her. The novel is again concerned with relative fortunes, examining the issue of female dependency through the portrayals of Harriet Smith, Jane Fairfax, Mrs Weston and Miss Bates. Its imaginative focus, however, remains firmly fixed on Emma Woodhouse, whose personal wealth means that she is free of the economic obligation to marry that influenced so many of Jane Austen's earlier characters. 'I have none of the usual inducements of women to marry,' she tells Harriet: 'Fortune I do not want; employment I do not want; consequence I do not want; I believe few married women are half as much mistress of their husband's house, as I am of Hartfield.' Emma's eloquence on the subject is as startling to readers of Jane Austen's earlier novels as it is to Harriet Smith. She is an entirely new kind of heroine and has unsettled readers ever since her first appearance in December 1815.

Despite Emma's sense of her own independence, she is nevertheless as preoccupied with the question of marriage as any of her predecessors. It is just that she does not restrict the matter to her own future. The novel opens on the evening of her governess's wedding, which Emma takes personal pride in having brought about ('I made the match, you know'). Within a couple of chapters, she has begun directing her matchmaking skills at Harriet Smith, whose sequence of infatuations and disappointments provides one of the main strands of the narrative. Emma's determined search for prospective husbands for Harriet and simultaneous denial of her own attraction to men shows Jane Austen's acute insight into the psychology of displaced desire. Much of the comedy and ultimate satisfaction of the novel arises from Emma's apparently endless misunderstanding, and eventual recognition, of her true feelings. The combination of the heroine's abundant self-confidence and unerring capacity to misread situations provides a new kind of comedy in which the witty woman can also be the butt of many jokes.

Jane Austen had already made much of the comic potential of the matchmaker in *Pride and Prejudice*, but Mrs Bennet's energy is contained within set dialogues and situations, her thoughts visible only from her speeches. Emma, however, has both the freedom to create her own romances and the will to extend her managerial powers into the lives of all those around her. At times, she is almost like a novelist within her own novel, as she conjures up suitors for Harriet and ignores the reality of her friend's situation, attractions or feelings. She is proud of being an 'imaginist', ever ready to be 'on fire with speculation and foresight', and so the slightest information rapidly assumes dramatic significance in her eager mind. Minor incidents are magnified and preserved in Emma's imagination, and her desire to turn life into fiction is abundantly apparent in her constant recital of 'the story of Harriet and the gipsies'.

If *Northanger Abbey* had considered the relationship between reading fiction and interpreting immediate experience, *Emma* extended the field to explore the very nature of imaginative creation. Jane Austen's perennial enjoyment of playing with literary convention was emerging in far more subtle ways, with the elaborate Gothic parody of the past condensed into passing jokes about Emma's fear of Miss Bates 'haunting the Abbey'. Her interest was now focused not so much on how to write successful fiction (a problem she had already solved), but on the very sources and processes of creative thought. By developing a narrative technique that allowed readers to share the heroine's perspective on a scene, even without the help of dialogue, Jane Austen was able to represent the workings of Emma's mind with far greater complexity than she had previously afforded her characters. At times, she offers Emma's thoughts as direct internal speech: ' "There is no charm equal to tenderness of heart," said she afterwards to herself.' At other moments, she develops the brilliant free indirect style that allows the omniscient narrator to recede and Emma's thoughts to take over, almost imperceptibly: 'Emma, beginning hastily and with an arch look, but soon stopping – it was better, however, to know the worst at once – . . .'

The novel's focus on the heroine also allows for detailed development of the growth of consciousness, so readers are able to trace the progress of, for instance, the 'ingenious and animating suspicion' that enters Emma's brain after an offhand remark by Miss Bates about her niece's friendship with the Dixons. As the idea is nourished by Jane Fairfax's subsequent reticence and Frank Churchill's interest, the imagined tendresse becomes more real to Emma than much of what is actually going on before her eyes. Jane Austen's attention to the stories that take hold of Emma's mind in this way affords remarkable insight into the imaginative process. Emma does not read the world through library books like Catherine Morland, but her imaginative response is just as powerful, and often just as misleading. Since Emma's sources lie not in the Gothic novels of the past, but in her immediate circle, she is a character to whom everyone can still relate, and whose mistakes are inevitably shared. For, while many readers see through her confusions over Mr Dixon at once, few can avoid responding with some impatience to Miss Bates's long speeches, and, as a consequence, are almost as thrown by discovering the limitations of their own judgement as Emma is after the visit to Box Hill.

If Emma's imagination leads to mistakes, however, it is also what makes her such a life-affirming character. Her father's habit of offering only very small portions of the plainest food to his guests is countered by Emma's generous spirit and her 'pleasure in sending them away happy'. Her sense of independence and her imaginative freedom enable her to make gifts and generate happiness, even if her attempts are not always sufficiently attentive to alternative views. Emma's relish for life means that she possesses a rare capacity for contentment. The little scene in Highbury in which she waits for Harriet to choose her muslin demonstrates that the benefits of Emma's imagination far outweigh any of its drawbacks:

> [W]hen her eyes fell only on the butcher with his tray, a tidy old woman travelling homewards from shop with her full basket, two curs quarrelling over a dirty bone, and a string of dawdling children round the baker's little bow-window eyeing the gingerbread, she knew she had no reason to complain, and was amused enough.

In a situation that might have nothing to interest the Bertrams or the Crawfords, Emma is perfectly happy. Anything can provide the materials for a new story, as long as the onlooker has a mind to create.

In *Emma*, Jane Austen was celebrating the power of the human imagination and demonstrating the riches of a rural environment. If her earlier novels had made jokes at the expense of Lady Susan or Caroline Bingley, with their prejudices against country towns and villages, *Emma* defended provincial life by revealing its untold imaginative wealth. Gilbert White, whose bestselling *Natural History of Selborne*, published in 1789, had already shown the world that his tiny Hampshire village, only four miles from Chawton, was a place of unique importance. Jane Austen similarly presented Highbury as the hub of the world, but her most remarkable achievement lay in creating a fictional place that was every bit as complete and convincing as her neighbour's factual record of his parish. Frank Churchill may joke about becoming a 'true citizen of Highbury' by buying gloves at Ford's, but his gently patronising tone is roundly answered by Mr Knightley's contempt for a man who would travel all the way to London for a haircut. Mr Knightley's relief at riding home after staying on in London, 'vigorously, day after day', is a telling inversion of the kinds of metropolitan prejudice encountered by Jane Austen on her visits to Henry in Chelsea. It may take time to understand the true value of Highbury, but many readers have discovered over the years that the world of *Emma* lives on in their minds with far greater vitality than many of the real places they have known.

Emma was not, after all, an inappropriate gift for the Prince Regent. Its patriotism is apparent in Emma's paean of praise to Donwell Abbey and Abbey-Mill Farm: 'It was a sweet view – sweet to the eye and the mind. English verdure, English culture, English comfort, seen under a sun bright, without being oppressive.' What need was there to travel abroad with such delights to be found on one's doorstep? The hidden heart of England was open to anyone who took the time to stop and look. *Emma*'s celebratory tone undoubtedly owes something to the national sense of relief at Napoleon's defeat and the banishment of long-standing fears about a French invasion, but the novel also reflects Jane Austen's deep gratitude for the quiet countryside that had proven so congenial to her creative spirit. In a letter offering advice to James Austen's daughter Anna, who was writing a novel of her own in 1814, Aunt Jane congratulated the young woman on setting the scene in 'such a spot as is the delight of my life; – 3 or 4 families in a Country Village is the very thing to work on'.[53] It was the very kind of spot in which Austen was now happiest because it worked so well – and therefore she could too. In *Mansfield Park*, she had examined the idea of a true home, but in *Emma* she knew that she had found one, and her happiness fills the novel.

Emma may be a flawed heroine, and, at times, her 'solitary grandeur' makes her seem melancholy despite all the blessings of her existence, but the novel is infused with a deep satisfaction. It is Jane Austen's most complicated creation, with a huge cast of brilliantly realised characters and a host of minor figures whose presence contributes to the overall sense of completion. The varied comedy of misunderstanding and game-playing, eccentricity and prejudice, snobbery and hypochondria, misplaced affection and rejected addresses is woven into a fine structure that is at once extraordinarily intricate and strong. Everything is so perfectly placed that it seems to follow as naturally and inevitably as the seasons, despite the complexity of the plot. Emma's vital freedom is possible *because* her world is so carefully grounded. Jane Austen was demonstrating the importance of attending to the tiniest parts, as well as their essential and cumulative contribution to the larger entity. As a healthy example for the future King of England, *Emma* could hardly have been better.

PERSUASION

1816

In *Emma*, Jane Austen resolved so many of the problems she had set for herself that she inadvertently created a new one: what could she write next? Such a virtuoso performance was not easy to follow, even for a writer whose voice had now achieved its perfect pitch. Once her authorship became known, she began to receive ideas from admirers such as James Stanier Clarke, the Prince Regent's librarian, who wrote on 16 November 1815 to suggest that she might turn her talents to delineating 'the Habits of Life and Character and enthusiasm of a Clergyman – who should pass his time between the metropolis & the Country – who should be something like Beatties Minstrel'. Although she politely demurred, claiming that she might be equal to the 'comic part of the

Character ... but not the Good, the Enthusiastic, the Literary',[54] Mr Clarke continued to send suggestions. By December, he was even imagining the clergyman being sent to sea 'as the Friend of some distinguished Naval Character about a Court'.[55] When he wrote again in March, urging her to compose a 'Historical Romance illustrative of the august House of Cobourg', it was time to make herself plain: 'I could not sit seriously down to write a serious Romance under any other motive than to save my Life,' she replied, '& if it were indispensable for me to keep it up & never relax into laughing at myself or other people, I am sure I should be hung before I had finished the first Chapter.'[56] She did not send Mr Clarke the hilarious 'Plan of a Novel', which his well-meaning but ill-judged ideas had provoked.[57]

Although Jane Austen modestly stressed her literary limitations and incurably comic inclinations, the correspondence with the Prince Regent's household displays the same underlying confidence that shines from every line of *Emma*. 'No – I must keep to my own style & go on in my own Way,' she wrote to Clarke – and, even though the letter is dated 1 April 1816, she clearly meant what she said. For that very day she also wrote to John Murray, thanking him for sending her a copy of the *Quarterly Review* that carried a long critical discussion of her work by no less a master than Walter Scott.

An author who was receiving serious public praise in one of the most influential literary journals had no need of advice on the subject of her next book, however well intended. She had spent long enough doubting the success of her work and had lost out on the copyright of *Pride and Prejudice* as a result. With the publication of *Emma*, she had found a new publisher and better terms, so she was not going to resume any deferential attitude. Indeed, in the early months of 1816, she had the satisfaction of recovering the old manuscript of 'Susan' from Crosby, revealing the identity of the work's anonymous author just as the *Quarterly* put its seal on her fame. By this point, however, Jane Austen was not prepared to publish work unless it met the exceptionally high standard she had achieved in *Emma*, and so, although she went back to 'Susan', renaming her novel 'Catherine' and making various related alterations, she was no longer satisfied with her earlier work. In March 1817, she wrote to her niece Fanny admitting that 'Miss Catherine is put upon the Shelve for the present, and I do not know that she will ever come out'.[58] The same letter nevertheless reveals in confidence that Austen had, after all, been working with much greater success on another project: 'I have a something ready for Publication, which may perhaps appear in about a twelvemonth hence.' That 'something' was *Persuasion*.

Although Jane Austen had made a start on the new novel soon after completing *Emma* in March 1815, she had largely managed to keep her work quiet. It had been a year of upheavals, with Napoleon's final attempt to regain power and his defeat at Waterloo providing the remarkable international prelude to Henry's near-fatal illness in the autumn and the subsequent collapse of his bank. Henry's bankruptcy had a great impact on the entire family, not only in their natural sympathy for his distresses, but also because Frank was a partner in the bank too, and so the financial repercussions for everyone were considerable. Charles was still far away in the eastern Mediterranean, but he seemed to take his share of the family's misfortunes when his ship was wrecked in a storm in the Aegean. Though exonerated from all blame, Charles came home depressed and poor, taking years to recover professionally from the disgrace of losing a ship. Worst of all, though not recognised as such at the time, Jane's health was beginning to decline. She began suffering from a bad back and deep fatigue during the summer of 1816 and, despite cheerful references to her recovery in letters that winter, she was evidently aware that something was not right.

The national rejoicing that accompanied the end of the war was evident in the buoyant mood of *Emma*, but by 1816 it seemed to be giving way to an all-engulfing depression. Nevertheless, in between attending to Henry in his London sickbed, supporting her mother through the family trials, and entertaining the extended family during their numerous visits to Chawton, Jane Austen succeeded in writing a novel every bit as innovative as *Emma*. Although she had told Mr Clarke that she must keep to her own style, this did not merely mean repeating her earlier successes. In *Persuasion*, she reconsidered many aspects of her previous novels, but the result was something quite unlike any of them.

With its West Country setting and initial focus on the loss of the family home, *Persuasion* is reminiscent of *Sense and Sensibility*, though the later section in Bath, perhaps influenced by the recovery of the 'Susan' manuscript from Crosby, has more in common with *Northanger Abbey*. The opening chapters, with their satirical portrayal of Sir Walter Elliot, also recall the embarrassing parents and exaggerated comic characters of *Pride and Prejudice*. Sir Walter's daughters have reached the age at which Charlotte Lucas deemed it prudent to accept Mr Collins, and so the pressure to find a husband, which afflicts so many of Austen's female precursors to Emma, is once again under scrutiny. At the same time, the interest in a baronet's household, his extravagant expenditure and the effect of external influence on domestic decisions seem more akin to *Mansfield Park*, especially since aristocratic assumptions about the world are so clearly contrasted with those of the navy. The symbolic transfer of Kellynch Hall from a flawed baronet to a capable naval commander seems a natural development from *Mansfield Park*; in replacing Lieutenant Price's noisy house with the admirable domesticity of Captain Harville and Admiral Croft, Jane Austen was extending her affectionate tribute to Frank and Charles, just when they needed it most.

If *Persuasion* reconsiders almost every major theme from the earlier novels, however, it is most indebted stylistically to *Emma*. *Persuasion* is a personal book in a way that none of the others are, but its private quality is achieved through the intense concentration on the mind of its heroine. In *Emma*, Jane Austen developed ways of presenting the narrative largely from the perspective of the central character, creating passages in which Emma's thoughts dominate the narrative interest, and even restricting much of the novel's dialogue to the subject of Emma. *Persuasion*, too, moves rapidly from the external portrayal of Sir Walter and his selfish obsessions to the secret inner life of his middle daughter. Anne Elliot may be disregarded by her family, but to readers, what goes on in her mind is far more compelling than what comes out of her father's mouth. The drama in *Persuasion* is psychological, as the entire novel reflects the peculiarly sensitive interior of the heroine. Where Emma's thoughts are often quick and decisive, reflected in short sentences, broken by dashes or exclamation marks, Anne Elliot's restrained contemplation is represented by long, beautifully controlled sentences that can run on for ten lines at a time. Even the passages of more detached narration retain an affinity to Anne's perception by adopting similar sentence patterns:

> They were come too late in the year for any amusement or variety which Lyme, as a public place, might offer; the rooms were shut up, the lodgers almost all gone, scarcely any family but of the residents left – and, as there is nothing to admire in the buildings themselves, the remarkable situation of the town, the principal street almost hurrying into the water, the walk to the Cobb, skirting round the pleasant little bay, which in the season is animated with bathing machines and company, the Cobb itself, its old wonders and new improvements, with the very beautiful line of cliffs stretching out to the east of the town, are what the stranger's eye will seek; and a very strange stranger it must be, who does not see the charms in the immediate environs of Lyme, to make him wish to know it better.

This striking paragraph carries all the conviction of first-hand experience and is obviously drawn from Jane Austen's memories of holidays in the Dorset resort in 1803 and 1804. Although the detail impresses the reality of the place on the page, its muted tone conveys the thoughtfulness of retrospect, of someone who understands what it means to feel that she has come too late. The bathing machines Jane Austen used when she spent all day swimming in the little bay had been packed away, and the impulse to retrieve them imaginatively – to relive remembered pleasures – was checked by the cool knowledge that that time was past, and all its aching joys were now no more. *Persuasion* nevertheless demonstrates the abundant artistic recompense derived from acknowledging the very difference.

Though much indebted to the innovations of *Emma*, reflective passages, such as the description of Lyme, distinguish *Persuasion* from the earlier novels, while also demonstrating that the very process of reconsidering them has paved the way to new achievement. When Jane Austen observed that 'these places must be visited, and visited again, to make the worth of Lyme understood', she was writing from her own experience – not just of Lyme itself, but of intense imaginative visiting and recollection. After completing *Emma*, she was returning to her personal and literary past. *Persuasion* is at once nostalgic and experimental, its unique character arising from the perpetual interaction between the sense of then and now, and from quiet, though often painful, reflection on the changes.

Persuasion is the first novel in which Jane Austen makes the past a crucial part of her narrative, impressing its importance from the opening chapter. Sir Walter Elliot's obsession with his family tree and Elizabeth Elliot's 'consciousness of being nine-and-twenty', with thirteen years of presiding over Kellynch Hall behind her, prepare the way for the real focus of the novel: Anne's preoccupation with her own unhappy history. At twenty-seven, Anne is older than any of the heroines in the earlier novels. Unlike her predecessors, her character has been formed by experiences that are not narrated directly. Whereas Emma enjoyed her teenage years with very little to distress or vex her, Anne Elliot's were marked by loss and loneliness. The successive blows of her mother's death and her broken engagement take place before the novel begins, and so the narrative is perpetually gazing backwards at the months of intense happiness, as well as the prolonged grief that occupies so much of Anne's internal experience.

Emma is also kept entirely free of dates, while *Persuasion* announces the dates of birth of the principal characters on the first page, and is then so specific about their ages that it is very clear to readers that the action of the novel takes place in 1814. The 'short period of exquisite felicity' enjoyed by Anne in the company of Captain Wentworth took place in 1806, a summer made all the more golden by its contrast with the surrounding years of warfare. Though Jane Austen had made passing references to public events in her previous novels, she had never before set the lives of her fictional characters so firmly against the great dramatic backdrop of her own turbulent times. Anne Elliot's sufferings are of a kind that anyone bereft and broken-hearted might experience, but they achieve a greater intensity through the additional fears relating to international conflict. When her fiancé left the country after their engagement was ended, he went off to a war in which his chances of survival were very uncertain. If *Emma* had caught the joyful mood of the moment of national peace, *Persuasion* reflected on the long years of anxiety that had preceded it.

As Jane Austen allowed her pen to dwell on feelings of misery in a way that she had never done before, she was establishing the most remarkable aspect of *Persuasion*: its almost imperceptible change of mood. If, at the beginning of the novel, Anne seems virtually paralysed by the distressing burden that has weighed on her for so many years, by the end she is staggered by 'an overpowering happiness'. The satisfaction of the novel's conclusion is greatly enriched by the sensitivity with which the heroine's feelings have been traced from dull depression, through moments of extreme pain, to a dawning capacity for amusement and a slowly recovering self-confidence, until hope and the possibility of fulfilment become real again at last. The scene at the White Hart, which Jane Austen carefully rewrote after rejecting the first ending she had conceived, is perhaps the most powerful emotional moment in her entire oeuvre. It is certainly one of the most complicated and sophisticated chapters, with its extraordinary control of a roomful of characters engaging in different conversations, each of which carries additional resonances for Anne and Wentworth, though they do not exchange a word. In the end, Jane Austen reverted to the device she had loved as a girl – the fictional letter. Where, in her youth, she had invariably made fun of the written declaration and used her epistles as a medium for parody, she now allowed Captain Wentworth to compose the most passionate address without a trace of irony. At forty, it seems, Jane Austen was prepared to lay down her comic defences when the situation demanded and allow unalloyed feeling to burst out across the page. No wonder that Anne Elliot is stunned, and those around her momentarily at a loss.

Persuasion is barely two-thirds of the length of *Emma*, and yet its slim form contains the greatest extremes of emotion, the most striking contrasts in narrative tone, the widest spectrum of social classes, the longest sweep of time and the most ambitious connections between the domestic and the national of any of her novels. Though most concise in its dealings with minor characters, it is the most generous in its development of the heroine. Though the most preoccupied with location, it also seems the most displaced of all. While each of the earlier novels sent their heroine on a significant journey, they also allowed her to return home, enlightened by her travels, whereas when Anne returns to Kellynch, she realises that her home has 'passed into better hands than its owners', and recognises that her expulsion is permanent.

It is only as she begins to look forwards rather than backwards, however, that the hints of an internal transformation can be fully realised. Once she has revisited Kellynch and seen that the world is not contained there, but lies all before her, Anne is ready to be restored to her true self. She learns from the past as she is liberated from its more restrictive influence, becoming ready to embrace new life, wherever it may take her. The openness of Anne's future, in comparison with the carefully located heroines of the earlier novels, is entirely consistent with the flexibility of *Persuasion*. She may be without her familiar habits and circle, but, in her new freedom, she is intensely happy. Jane Austen, too, had discovered hidden strengths in the course of writing *Persuasion* and, as she put down her pen in July 1816, seemed poised for future greatness. The emotional honesty of the book is such, however, that it also succeeds in conveying a dim sense that the happiness being celebrated so warmly is perhaps wishful thinking.

'WINCHESTER RACES'

1817

Jane Austen had no illusions about mortality. By 1817, she had seen the lives of two first cousins, three sisters-in-law, her sister's fiancé and her cousin's husband all cut short. She had lost her father and mourned the deaths of aunts and friends. Her letters are scattered with references to stillbirths and miscarriages, to mothers who died in labour and to infants who succumbed soon afterwards. She had nursed both her mother and her elder brother through illnesses that had nearly carried them off; she was even now hoping for an end to the suffering of her little niece Harriet, whose mysterious brain disease was driving Charles Austen to distraction. In her novels, however, death is never described directly, figuring largely as a plot device to bring about an enabling change for the surviving characters. There are moments when death seems uncomfortably close – in Marianne Dashwood's sick chamber, at Mansfield Park during Tom Bertram's fever, on the hard stone of the Cobb in *Persuasion* – but, in each case, death is warded off, the mood lightens and the story continues. Much of the time, illness provides comedy: Mrs Bennet's nerves and Mr Woodhouse's worries are there to make us laugh rather than cry. As Jane Austen's own symptoms became more severe, she might have decided to abandon her writing and rest. Instead, she embarked on a new novel that satirised contemporary medicine.

In *Persuasion*, she had recalled the Dorset shoreline with remarkable passages of lyrical beauty, but in *Sanditon* the sea breezes are more biting. The little Sussex village that has suddenly been 'planned & built, & praised & puffed, & raised . . . to a Something of young Renown' by Mr Parker could hardly be more different from the wistful evocations of Lyme Regis.[59] The cool comment on the fleeting nature of fame encapsulated in Mr Parker's regret over his choice of 'Trafalgar House' for his new establishment ('for Waterloo is more the thing now') seems to anticipate the spirit of Byron's new poem *Don Juan* rather than to recall Wordsworth's 'Tintern Abbey'. In *Persuasion*, the satire had broken open to reveal the romantic yearning within, but *Sanditon*, even in its fragmentary form, reveals little sign of deep emotion beneath the rapid conversations about bilious attacks and rheumatism. In *Emma*, the relative merits of South End and Cromer are debated in the brilliant comic scene in which Mr Woodhouse and John Knightley are each determined to demonstrate the superiority of their own doctor. In *Sanditon*, the medical humour is much less subtle, shooting out in Mr Parker's ludicrous enthusiasm for Sanditon's fresh air and deep water: 'They were antispasmodic, anti-pulmonary, anti-septic, anti-bilious & anti-rheumatic. Nobody could catch cold by the Sea. Nobody wanted Appetite by the Sea, Nobody wanted Spirits, Nobody wanted Strength.' The very things that Jane Austen most wanted, in fact, were being offered as hollow promises in the determinedly comic novel she was struggling to write. Even Sir Edward Denham's very funny attempts to seduce Charlotte by quoting the poetry of Burns are poignantly ironic, since Burns himself died of a fever developed after medical attempts to treat his life-threatening illness sent him sea-bathing in the Solway Firth. Beneath the comedy of *Sanditon* runs the knowledge that, whatever energy, money or hope human beings might invest in medical treatment, they will always be confronted in the end with the truth of their own mortality. Even when Mr Parker is at his most persuasive, his enthusiasm is quietly punctured when he announces that sea air and bathing are 'nearly infallible'.

In letters written during the early months of 1817, Jane Austen maintained the same resolutely cheerful front, reassuring Fanny that she was 'tolerably well again, quite equal to walking about & enjoying the Air', but her health was failing all the time.[60] By May, the apothecary in Alton had given up on attempting to cure the violent attacks and overwhelming exhaustion that had seized her, and so Mr Lyford, a first-class surgeon from Winchester, was called to Chawton. Since it is clear, with hindsight, that she was in the grip of either Addison's disease or some form of cancer, any improvement could only be a temporary respite. What the Austens saw, however, was what they wanted to see – that Mr Lyford had worked wonders and 'gradually removed the Evil', and that Jane should therefore go to Winchester to continue receiving his care.[61] Her old friends Elizabeth and Alethea Bigg, who were now living in the cathedral close, found a pretty house in College Street for the Austen sisters to stay until Jane recovered. 'I am now really a very genteel, portable sort of an Invalid,' she observed in May, when faced with the prospect of being bumped along the sixteen-mile journey by carriage.[62] Still she maintained her faith that 'the Providence of God' had restored her to better health, adding, with a characteristic blend of wit and humility, '& may I be more fit to appear before him when I *am* summoned, than I shd have been now!'.

The house overlooked the headmaster's garden at Winchester College, and she could hear the shouts of schoolboys through the bow window. Across the street, at the front, was the great grey wall of the close, built of flint and meant to last for ever. The chimes from the massive cathedral helped to order her prayers and calm her spirits. Although the doctors continued to be encouraging, Jane Austen knew well that her condition was serious and she was making appropriate preparations. She had made a will on 27 April, several weeks before the move to Winchester and, apart from a few small gifts, had left everything to her 'tender, watchful, indefatigable nurse', Cassandra.[63] When she thought of what she owed to her sister and 'to the anxious affection of all' her beloved family, she confessed, 'I can only cry over it, and pray to God to bless them more.'[64] Six weeks after expressing these feelings, she suffered another attack that left her barely conscious. She died two days later, at half past four in the morning of Thursday 18 July 1817.

For Cassandra, Jane's death was devastating. 'She was the sun of my life,' she wrote three days later, 'it is as if I had lost a part of myself.'[65] The funeral, attended by Edward, Henry, Frank and James's eldest son, James Edward, took place early on Thursday 24 July in order to be over by the time the first service began in the cathedral. The sense of loss that convulsed the Austens is preserved on the large black tombstone in the floor of Winchester Cathedral, which states that 'their grief is in proportion to their affection' and that 'they know their loss to be irreparable'. The moving inscription speaks of the 'benevolence of her heart, the sweetness of her temper, the extraordinary endowments of her mind' and the 'warmest love' Jane Austen inspired in those closest to her. But it makes no mention of her writing.

Although the monument seems to represent the final statement, the last words composed by Jane Austen herself adopted a rather different tone. Three days before she died, she dictated a poem to Cassandra. By now, her mind was on the cathedral – the tombs and the prayers, the vaulted ceilings and the arching aisles, the shrine of St Swithin behind the high altar. Rather than composing a devotional lyric, however, Jane Austen's imagination was playing over the old legend of St Swithin's Day – if it rains on 15 July, it will rain for forty days afterwards. The story has its origins in St Swithin's canonisation, which took place on 15 July 971, when his bones were moved from the old grave outside to a new shrine within the cathedral. As Jane Austen lay dying on St Swithin's Day 1817, she noticed that the Winchester races were taking place that very day, and she was struck by what 'the old Saint' might think of the fashionable parade at the race meeting. Though her body was weak, her mind was still capable of imaginative leaps, as the description of St Swithin springing from his shrine to address the Winchester racegoers from the cathedral roof proves:

> 'Oh, subjects rebellious, Oh Venta depraved
> When once we are buried you think we are dead
> But behold me Immortal. – By vice you're enslaved
> You have sinn'd & must suffer. – Then further he said
>
> These races & revels & dissolute measures
> With which you're debasing a neighbouring Plain
> Let them stand – you shall meet with your curse in
>   your pleasures
> Set off for your course, I'll pursue with my rain.
>
> Ye cannot but know my command o'er July
> Henceforward I'll triumph in shewing my powers
> Shift your race as you will it shall never be dry
> The curse upon Venta is July in showers.'[66]

Jane Austen's last work, characteristically enough, is a comic poem about the English weather.

REMEMBERING JANE

'B ehold me immortal!' When Jane Austen imagined St Swithin's refusal to lie down and be forgotten, she probably did not feel as confident about her own long-term survival. For all her contemporary success, in 1817 her chosen genre was still regarded as relatively minor and was yet to achieve recognition as serious literature. During the nineteenth century, as the novel grew in stature, so did Jane Austen's literary standing. Despite the incomprehension of readers like Charlotte Brontë, Austen's novels continued to be enjoyed and increasingly attracted a powerful body of influential admirers. For George Henry Lewes, the well-known writer, editor, reviewer and partner of George Eliot, there was no question of Jane Austen's work being forgotten, as he announced to readers of *Blackwood's Edinburgh*

Magazine in 1859: 'Such art as hers can never grow old, can never be superseded.'[67] His prediction has proven true. By the end of the nineteenth century, Jane Austen's novels were appearing in numerous editions, often beautifully bound and illustrated, while the foremost critics of the day were describing her as the Shakespeare of English prose. There were even special words for her supporters: the *Oxford English Dictionary* records the use of 'Janeite' as early as 1896, with 'Austenite' and 'Austenian' being coined in the early twentieth century as the numbers devoted to her work and memory continued to grow.

Interest in Jane Austen's own life was stimulated initially by the brief but affectionate 'Biographical Notice' written by her brother Henry to accompany *Northanger Abbey* and *Persuasion* when they were published together a few months after her death. He revised the short, but important, account when all the novels were brought out as a set in 1833. But it was not until 1870 that the first substantial biography appeared, written by James Austen's son James Edward Austen-Leigh, one of the pallbearers at his aunt's funeral in 1817, who felt duty-bound to collect any surviving family memories to compile a suitable tribute. *A Memoir of Jane Austen* stimulated renewed interest in the novels, especially when it reappeared in 1871 with fresh material, including the startling tale of 'Lady Susan'. Despite introducing Victorian readers to the unabashed amorality of Lady Susan, the *Memoir* also established a clear image of the novelist herself – as a retiring maiden aunt, living quietly with her mother and sister in a tiny country village. As critical interest in Austen's work became more serious, the popular idea of Jane Austen's rural England, filled with pretty girls in pretty gowns and a life untroubled by anything more difficult than the choice of dress or dancing partner, began to take root. The enduring appeal of Austen's work to numerous readers found permanent form a century after her death when, amid the devastation of the First World War, supporters from Britain and America commissioned a memorial tablet for Jane Austen's home at Chawton. Soon after the war, R. W. Chapman began work on the first scholarly edition of Jane Austen's novels, published by Oxford University Press in 1923. Her status as a major author was now beyond doubt, and Chapman's edition provided a sound basis for the studies of her work and for the paperback editions that poured from numerous presses in the following decades. Jane Austen had the honour of being 'the first modern novelist' conferred on her by F. R. Leavis, whose confident judgements influenced a whole generation of younger scholars and writers. When Ian Watt published his seminal *The Rise of the Novel* in 1957, Jane Austen was singled out as the culmination of eighteenth-century experimentation and the inaugurator of the great English novel of the nineteenth century. At a time when women writers seemed to be slipping out of critical sight, Jane Austen's reputation remained secure. As feminist critics in the late 1970s and '80s began to challenge the male domination of the literary canon, Jane Austen, though hardly in need of rescue, received a wave of new attention from readers who especially admired her clear treatment of issues relating to women. Familiar assumptions about the novels were overturned by critics who saw a figure such as Emma Woodhouse not as a flawed heroine in need of careful correction, but as an icon of female empowerment. At the same time, sharpened awareness of the historical contexts in which Austen wrote meant that readers were more alert to issues such as slavery in *Mansfield Park*, or to the political implications of her great estates and naval characters.

While academic debates have raged over Jane Austen's politics or lack of political awareness, the wider enthusiasm for her work has continued unabated. The development of film and television in the twentieth century provided an entirely new stage for Jane Austen's characters, many of whom are now initially encountered on screens rather than pages. Aldous Huxley wrote the screenplay for the first cinematic adaptation of *Pride and Prejudice* in 1940, and the BBC made a pioneering production of *Emma* in 1948. Since then, Jane Austen has remained a staple of television costume drama, and from the 1990s onwards, her novels have been transformed into a bewildering sequence of lavish offerings, attracting the most celebrated actors and producers. In 1995 alone, Kate Winslet made her name as Marianne Dashwood in Ang Lee's *Sense and Sensibility*, Amanda Root gave a brilliant performance as Anne Elliot in Roger Michell's *Persuasion*, Amy Heckerling interpreted *Emma* for the cult teen movie *Clueless*, and Andrew Davies's six-part adaptation of *Pride and Prejudice* fixed the image of a dripping Mr Darcy in the minds of millions of BBC viewers. The appetite for watching Jane Austen's stories seems unappeasable, every year bringing new versions to compete with those already in circulation.

Film-makers have not limited themselves to adapting the novels. Jane Austen's life has also caught the imagination of audiences around the world, providing the inspiration for *Becoming Jane* in 2007. James Edward Austen-Leigh and his sisters would probably have been surprised by this twenty-first-century Hollywood treatment of their aunt, who is embodied in the beautiful form of Anne Hathaway and depicted in the grip of a mutual passion. As such, the Jane Austen of contemporary imagination is youthful, confident and energetic, equally handy with a cricket bat as with a pen. She cuts quite a different figure from the late-Victorian Miss Austen, with her neat little writing desk and exquisite needlecraft. Each generation creates its idea of Jane Austen, who lives for ever in her own books. Over two centuries have passed since her words were first heard through the printed pages of *Sense and Sensibility*. But, far from becoming fainter with the passage of time, her voice, if altering at all, has grown stronger and clearer as the years have gone by.

AFTERWORD

When Jane Austen spoke of being 'in love with' Clarkson, in a private letter of 1813, she was referring to the indefatigable anti-slavery campaigner Thomas Clarkson and his splendid *History*, which charted the progress of the abolitionist movement.[68] Two hundred years later, the name of Clarkson would be linked very publicly to her own in a rather different kind of campaign. Once the news broke in 2012 that the American singer Kelly Clarkson was about to return to the United States with a ring belonging to Jane Austen, there was a national outcry in Britain. Clarkson had bought the ring entirely legitimately at an auction sale for £152,450, but so powerful was the wave of public feeling that the Culture Secretary felt obliged to impose a temporary export embargo, giving indignant supporters the chance to raise sufficient funds to save the ring for the nation. For many of her readers, the very idea of Jane Austen sporting a pretty gold and turquoise ring came as something of a surprise. Her novels are hardly gem-bespangled and, when an item of jewellery does appear, it is often a focus of attention – and tension. Edward Ferrars's arrival at Barton Cottage wearing a ring containing a lock of fair hair causes almost as much consternation as the gold necklaces given to Fanny Price in *Mansfield Park*. It was oddly appropriate, then, that the author's own ring should have generated such powerful feeling. Within a year, the money had been raised, Kelly Clarkson graciously withdrew her right of possession, and the ring went on display at the Jane Austen's House Museum in Chawton, where it remains. Ardent admirers can even buy a replica for £450.

If Jane Austen endured her painful last days by amusing herself with thoughts of St Swithin's reaction to his canonisation, she might (or might not) have been comforted by the knowledge that her own supporters would eventually come to regard her with similar reverence. Anything touched by Jane Austen is now treated almost as a religious relic: revered, coveted, contested and finally displayed at a shrine for pilgrims to wonder at. Chawton Cottage now attracts some 40,000 visitors a year, all wanting to see the bedroom in which she slept in, the donkey cart in which she travelled in, the little round table at which she sat and wrote. The gardener at Chawton even has to contend with devotees determined to scatter the ashes of loved ones on the earth where Jane Austen once walked. Her significance in English literary history has been abundantly evident since the beginning of the twentieth century, but her peculiar place in broader cultural life only became fully apparent towards its close. In the decade since the original version of this short biography was completed, Jane Austen's stature has assumed extraordinary proportions – and shows no sign of shrinking.

Famous authors inspire many different kinds of devotion, ranging from the serious scholarship of those whose lives are spent studying the work to the creative responses of artists and writers in every medium. Then there is the design and production of remarkably varied merchandise aimed at the largest band of followers: enthusiastic readers, viewers and visitors. 'Jane Austen' has long since ceased to refer solely to a woman novelist who lived between 1775 and 1817; it has expanded to encompass an icon and an industry.

As the twenty-first century rolled into its second decade, the bicentenary of Jane Austen's first published novel generated fresh interest in a novelist whose reputation was in need of no help. Celebrations of *Sense and Sensibility* set the scene for 2011, but it was a

2017

new portrait of Jane Austen that really stole the media attention, forming the centrepiece of the BBC's Austenfest on Boxing Day that year. Paula Byrne's identification of Jane Austen as the sitter in a Regency portrait she owned was a very significant development – not least because, until then, the only portrait known to have been taken from life was the little watercolour sketch by Cassandra. This slender, upright woman sitting in front of a window in Westminster was very different from the subject of the intimate sketch by Jane Austen's sister, but Paula Byrne was struck by the facial resemblance to portraits of the Austen brothers, an insight prompted by the name on the back of the picture: 'Jane Austin'. Her energetic and persuasive case for the authenticity of this newly discovered Austen portrait did not carry universal conviction, and probably will not unless the crucial question of provenance, essential for all firm attributions in the art world, is resolved. The picture nevertheless went on display at the Jane Austen's House Museum and was reproduced in Byrne's biography, *The Real Jane Austen: A Life in Small Things*.

An even more significant event for Austen scholars that year was the Bodleian Library's acquisition of the manuscript of 'The Watsons'. (The purchase also attracted considerable media attention, largely on account of the sum involved: £993,250.) Very little of Jane Austen's fiction survives in its original form, so this was a unique opportunity to secure an early, unfinished draft in Jane Austen's own handwriting. This precious remnant, like the unpublished *Sanditon*, similarly scored with crossings-out and second thoughts, offers rare insight into Austen's creative process, otherwise lost in the transition from manuscript to print. Hints in the letters and family anecdotes about the writer who firmly lopped and cropped her stories are fully corroborated by these brief but invaluable manuscript fragments.

There has never been any doubt about the importance of Austen's manuscripts, but it is only in the past decade that they have become accessible to a wide audience. Excitement over 'The Watsons' was fanned by an extraordinary website. Jane Austen's Fiction Manuscripts is an online resource launched in October 2010 that enables people all over the world to see what survives of the hand-written narratives, simply by visiting janeausten. ac.uk. Here are the three volumes of her juvenilia; here is the original ending of *Persuasion*; here is *Sanditon*, with no end in sight. Anyone can now take a look at the flourishes of her teenage quill that adorn the dedications and finales of early gifts to family members.

The digitisation of the fiction manuscripts, carried out by Kathryn Sutherland and her expert team, has made the potential of utilising electronic technology to enlarge understanding of the novels abundantly evident. The visual possibilities of computer graphics have also begun to open up other areas of Jane Austen's world. In May 1813, Jane Austen, flushed with excitement over the publication of *Pride and Prejudice*, was staying with her brother Henry and taking the opportunity to visit the London art galleries. At an exhibition put on by the Society of Painters in Oil and Watercolours, she was very pleased to spot a portrait resembling Jane Bennet: 'Mrs Bingley's is exactly herself, size, shaped face, features & sweetness; there never was a greater likeness. She is dressed in a white gown, with green ornaments, which convinces me of what I had always supposed, that green was a favourite colour with her.'[69] Jane Austen also supposed that 'Mrs D. will be in yellow', but the gallery failed to offer a suitable candidate. A few days later, at the Reynolds retrospective in Pall Mall, she was again disappointed to find no image matching her idea of Elizabeth Bennet ('I can only imagine that Mr D. prizes any Picture of her too much to like it should be exposed to the public eye'[70]). Her unsatisfactory search has now borne unexpected fruit in the form of a virtual reconstruction of the Reynolds exhibition of 1813. The What Jane Saw project, led by the Austen scholar Janine Barchas, allows present-day viewers to enter the gallery, admire the paintings and even move from room to room. They will not spot an image of Elizabeth Bennet, but they can at least find out what she did *not* look like, in the eyes of the ultimate authority.

The author often regarded as quintessentially English is now an international phenomenon, as immediate to those in the Antipodes as in Andover. The Jane Austen Society of the United Kingdom was founded in 1940, chiefly to help with the preservation of the Chawton home. It has since grown into a flourishing organisation with numerous members and meetings. Branches have spread across the British Isles; new societies continue to sprout all over the world. The Jane Austen Society of Pakistan meets annually in December for a birthday tea party, while the Jane Austen Society of Australia celebrates with a pre-Christmas lunch in Sydney. Spain is one of the more recent countries to launch a Jane Austen Society, now offering competitions, conversations and reading clubs, while the Jane Austen Society of North America (JASNA), founded in 1979, currently boasts some 5,000 members and seventy regional branches, as well as a reputation for exuberant annual meetings and an excellent online journal, Persuasions.

The bicentenary of *Pride and Prejudice* in 2013 was a global phenomenon, marked by a celebrity readathon in Bath, exhibitions in Canterbury, Chawton, Edinburgh, Gretna Green, London, Lyme Park, Oxford and Winchester, study days in Brighton, Chawton, London,

Oxford and York, and international conferences in Adelaide, Brisbane, Cambridge, Chicago, New York, Singapore and Tokyo. Regency balls and dinners abounded, Austen weekends became de rigueur, Cunard launched Austen-related transatlantic cruises. The Royal Mail entered into the mood of the moment by issuing a set of stamps to honour the occasion and designing a special postmark for letters sent from Chawton or Steventon in the publication anniversary week. Even the Bank of England did its bit to bolster Jane's fame. In the year of *Pride and Prejudice*, Governor Mark Carney announced that Jane Austen would be the face of the new £10 note, replacing Charles Darwin (who, as a great admirer of her novels, would probably have had no objection).

Jane Austen herself might well have been amused by Cassandra's little portrait being transformed into currency, as well as by the choice of accompanying quotation: 'I declare after all there is no enjoyment like reading!' She composed these words for Miss Bingley, whose preference, in fact, is more for banknotes than books. The portrayal of Jane Austen on a £10 note is in keeping with a view long held by certain critics that money was a major preoccupation for her. W. H. Auden's comment is the pithiest: in his 'Letter to Lord Byron', he confessed to being shocked to see 'An English spinster of the middle class . . . Reveal so frankly and with such sobriety / The economic basis of society.'[71] What would Auden have had to say about the handful of 'Jane Austen fivers' that began to circulate late in 2016, on which a tiny portrait of Austen engraved by Graham Short increased the notes' value to £50,000? Or about the auction in March 2017 at which a first edition of *Pride and Prejudice* sold for £38,000?

'Jane Austen' is big business. *Pride and Prejudice* has been précised and presented via kittens, knitted figures and guinea pigs dressed in bonnets and lace. There are peg doll kits and cut-out cards of Mr Darcy. Quotations from the novels have found their way onto bags, bookmarks and bracelets, mugs and mousemats, cushion covers and caps. Marketing opportunities are a sign of modern success, but the merchandise tells much about the enduring appeal of Jane Austen. Whatever earlier literary critics may have had to say about the transcendent truths embodied in her words, the memorabilia tells another story. The Jane Austen action figure, striding confidently ahead with pen in hand, is a different Jane from the late-Victorian image of the spinster aunt at her tiny table. What Lady Catherine de Bourgh offered as a crushing insult to Elizabeth Bennet is now sported proudly on T-shirts: 'Obstinate Headstrong Girl'.

Publishers have done their best to fuel Austen-mania, bringing out books aimed at stimulating more participation in the Regency world. Anyone wishing to throw their own version of the Netherfield ball can seek advice from books such as *Dinner with Mr Darcy*, *A Dance with Jane Austen* or *Regency Women's Dress*. There has also been a series of more traditional, academic studies of Jane Austen's texts, but twenty-first-century scholars are more willing than their predecessors to take into account the popular responses to those. The avalanche of Austen-related events, books, blogs and bric-à-brac has created a playful aura around an author at one time admired primarily for her moral vision. John Mullan's book of conundrums – *What Matters in Jane Austen?* – catches the tone in its title. Like John Sutherland's *Who Betrays Elizabeth Bennet?*, Mullan's collection of questions prompted by the novels combines critical expertise with a sense of fun, even adding a slightly more gossipy tone ('Is There Any Sex in Jane Austen?'). Unsurprisingly, the work that attracts most attention from Mullan is the one in which puzzles and charades are most prominent – *Emma*.

Fascination with Jane Austen's novels has led to the pursuit of puzzles of a very different kind. 'Who killed Fanny Price?' is the question posed by Lynn Shepherd in *Murder at Mansfield Park*, in which she takes a widely held readerly aversion to Austen's heroine to extremes by transforming *Mansfield Park* into crime fiction. Suddenly, Jane Austen is inadvertently revealed as the mother of the whodunnit, as well as everything else – the familiar genre of the country house murder, usually traced to Agatha Christie, is here found to derive from *Mansfield Park*. Or should that be *Pride and Prejudice*? P. D. James's *Death Comes to Pemberley* takes its cue from *Pride and Prejudice*, and has now become a bestselling crime novel and subsquent television adaptation. If these murder mysteries play fast and loose with Jane Austen, they are positively strait-laced in comparison to Seth Grahame-Smith's *Pride and Prejudice and Zombies* or Ben Winters's *Sense and Sensibility and Sea Monsters*. Austen herself was not averse to coining new words, as seen in Emma's idea of herself as 'an imaginist', so it is apt enough that she should have inspired a new genre of literary 'mash-up' (since the amalgamation of Pemberley and a zombie apocalypse had no obvious literary precedent, reviewers turned to the contemporary music scene to find an adequate term). *Pride and Prejudice and Zombies*, of course, was also destined for the big screen.

Though not to the taste of every Janeite, the mash-ups demonstrate, more than any other recent phenomenon, the extent to which Austen's stories have now achieved the status of modern myth, so widely known that they are open to being adapted, inverted or subverted. Even the distant offspring of her novels have assumed lives of their own. Helen Fielding's Bridget Jones first appeared in a newspaper column; her story, mirroring *Pride and Prejudice*, borrowed first the name of Austen's hero and then, for the cinematic version, the actor Colin Firth, who played Darcy in the BBC adaptation. *Bridget Jones's Diary* was followed by *Bridget Jones: The Edge of Reason* and, more recently, a film that fast-forwards a few years to *Bridget Jones's Baby*.

Since 2011, the bewildering succession of Jane Austen bicentenaries has brought home the concentration of her original output, each year giving rise to celebrations of another novel. Six great novels in the space of six years was – and still is – a remarkable achievement. The twenty-first-century obsession with anniversaries has also meant that the tributes to Jane Austen have coincided with commemorations of the First World War. Historical accident brought *Mansfield Park*, *Emma* and *Persuasion* into contact with the convulsions of the early twentieth century, and, in doing so, highlighted the conflict of Jane Austen's own day. The Napoleonic Wars may seem far removed from Mansfield or Highbury, but the appeal of these settings' tranquillity is greatly intensified by the thought of what so many contemporary brothers, husbands and sons were enduring and how their bereft sisters, wives and mothers were suffering. With images of the First World War so much in mind, the commemorative plaque commissioned by Jane Austen's supporters in 1917 for the centenary of her death takes on poignant additional dimensions. The black tablet, set into the brick wall of her home in Chawton, bears a striking resemblance to the memorials that were being erected in villages all over Britain in the wake of the vast battles of northern France. Lewes's prediction, uttered in more peaceful times, deepened into a statement of faith when it was engraved in brass and mounted on oak in 1917. It continues to provide a suitably enduring monument to Jane Austen: 'Such art as hers can never grow old'.

NOTES

1. *Jane Austen's Letters*, ed. Deirdre Le Faye, 4th edn (Oxford, 2011), p. 351.
2. The principal sources of information concerning Jane Austen's family are the memoirs and recollections written by her relatives. See: James Edward Austen-Leigh, *A Memoir of Jane Austen and Other Family Recollections*, ed. Kathryn Sutherland (Oxford, 2002); William Austen-Leigh and Richard Arthur Austen-Leigh, *Jane Austen: A Family Record*, ed. Deirdre Le Faye (London, 1989); Deirdre Le Faye, *Jane Austen: A Family Record* (Cambridge, 2004); and idem, *A Chronology of Jane Austen and her Family 1700–2000* (Cambridge, 2006). See also George Holbert Tucker's useful *A History of Jane Austen's Family*, rev. edn (Stroud, 1998).
3. *The Complete Poems of James Austen*, ed. David Selwyn (Chawton, 2003), p. 20.
4. Austen-Leigh, *Memoir*, p. 18.
5. The description is from 'The Letter of Sophia Sentiment', discussed in chapter two and included in *The Cambridge Edition of the Works of Jane Austen: Juvenilia*, ed. Peter Sabor (Cambridge, 2006), p. 361.
6. Gilbert White, *The Natural History of Selborne*, ed. Richard Mabey (Harmondsworth, 1977), p. 265.
7. *Juvenilia*, p. 362.

8. Ibid., pp. 3, 13.
9. Ibid., p. 54.
10. Ibid., p. 42.
11. Ibid., p. 51.
12. Ibid., p. 8.
13. Ibid., pp. 343, 323.
14. Ibid., p. 178.
15. Ibid., p. 220.
16. Ibid., p. 244.
17. *Jane Austen's Letters*, p. 31.
18. Ibid., p. 1.
19. Ibid., p. 2.
20. Ibid., p. 4.
21. Ibid., p. 71.
22. Ibid., pp. 31, 36.
23. Ibid., p. 20.
24. Ibid., p. 5.
25. Ibid., p. 41.
26. Ibid., p. 5.
27. 'Lady Susan', *The Works of Jane Austen: Volume VI, Minor Works*, ed. R. W. Chapman, rev. B. C. Southam (Oxford, 1969) p. 252.
28. Anna Lefroy, 'Recollections of Aunt Jane', Austen-Leigh, *Memoir*, p. 158.
29. *Jane Austen's Letters,* p. 41.
30. Ibid., p. 71.
31. Ibid.
32. Ibid., p. 27.
33. Ibid., p. 15.
34. Anthony Mandal, 'Making Austen Mad: Benjamin Crosby and the Non-Publication of "Susan" ', *RES*, ns 57 (2006), pp. 507–25.
35. 'The Watsons', *Minor Works*, p. 317.
36. Jon Spence's book *Becoming Jane Austen* (London, 2003) led to Julian Jarrold's 2007 blockbuster film, *Becoming Jane*.
37. Letter to James Edward Austen-Leigh, Austen-Leigh, *Memoir*, p. 188.
38. Henry Austen, 'Biographical Notice of the Author', Austen-Leigh, *Memoir*, p. 139.
39. Austen-Leight, *Memoir*, p. 70.
40. Caroline Austen, 'My Aunt Jane Austen: A Memoir', Austen-Leigh, *Memoir*, p. 169.
41. *Jane Austen's Letters*, p. 28.

42. The verse by Jane Austen's mother is published in full in W. R. and R. A. Austen-Leigh's *Family Record*, p. 125.
43. *Jane Austen's Letters*, p. 100.
44. Austen, *Complete Poems of James Austen*, p. 39.
45. *Jane Austen's Letters*, p. 212.
46. Ibid., p. 30.
47. Ibid., p. 190.
48. Ibid, p. 210.
49. Ibid.
50. Austen's assessment of Emma Woodhouse is recorded in Austen-Leigh, *Memoir*, p. 119.
51. *Jane Austen's Letters*, pp. 207, 216–17.
52. Ibid., p. 241.
53. Ibid., p. 287.
54. Ibid., p. 319.
55. Ibid., p. 320.
56. Ibid, pp. 325–6.
57. 'Plan of a Novel' is reproduced in *Minor Works*, pp. 428–30, and in *The Cambridge Edition of the Works of Jane Austen: Later Manuscripts*, ed. Janet Todd and Linda Bree (Cambridge, 2008), pp. 226–9.
58. *Jane Austen's Letters*, p. 348.
59. 'Sanditon', *Minor Works*, p. 371.
60. *Jane Austen's Letters*, p. 348.
61. Ibid., p. 356.
62. Ibid.
63. *Jane Austen's Letters*, pp. 355, 358.
64. Ibid.
65. Ibid., pp. 359–60.
66. The text is from *Later Manuscripts*, p. 255, and the editors' discussion of the surviving manuscripts (neither in Jane Austen's own hand) is on pp. 738–9.
67. G. H. Lewes, 'The Novels of Jane Austen', *Blackwood's Edinburgh Magazine*, lxxxvi (July 1859), pp. 99–113.
68. *Jane Austen's Letters*, p. 207.
69. Ibid., p. 221.
70. Ibid., p. 222.
71. W. H. Auden, 'Letter to Lord Byron', in W. H. Auden and Louis MacNeice, *Letters from Iceland* (London, 1937).

BIBLIOGRAPHY

A biography of this kind is inevitably indebted to the numerous studies of Jane Austen's life and works. The list below represents a selection of the most important sources. Many of these books will be of interest to those who wish to pursue their knowledge of Jane Austen beyond this brief life. When it comes to reading the novels, there are many good modern editions with reliable texts, helpful introductions and illuminating notes, such as those published in the new Penguin Classics, Oxford World's Classics, Norton Critical Editions or Harvard annotated Austen series, as well as *The Cambridge Edition of the Works of Jane Austen*. R. W. Chapman's edition of the novels is still widely available and always enjoyable.

Publications

Auden, W. H., and MacNeice, Louis, *Letters from Iceland* (London, 1937)

Austen, Caroline, *Reminiscences of Caroline Austen*, ed. Deirdre Le Faye (Chawton, 1986)

Austen, James, *The Complete Poems of James Austen*, ed. David Selwyn (Chawton, 2003)

Austen, Jane, *The Novels of Jane Austen*, ed. R. W. Chapman (1923), 3rd edn rev. Mary Lascelles, 5 vols (Oxford, 1965–9)

—, *The Works of Jane Austen: Volume VI, Minor Works*, ed. R. W. Chapman, rev. B. C. Southam (Oxford, 1969)

—, *The Cambridge Edition of the Works of Jane Austen: Juvenilia*, ed. Peter Sabor (Cambridge, 2006)

—, *The Cambridge Edition of the Works of Jane Austen: Later Manuscripts*, ed. Janet Todd and Linda Bree (Cambridge, 2008)

—, *Jane Austen's Letters*, ed. Deirdre Le Faye, 4th edn (Oxford, 2011)

Austen-Leigh, James Edward, *A Memoir of Jane Austen and Other Family Recollections*, ed. Kathryn Sutherland (Oxford, 2002)

Austen-Leigh, William and Richard Arthur, *Jane Austen: A Family Record*, ed. Deirdre Le Faye (London, 1989)

Barchas, Janine, *Matters of Fact in Jane Austen* (Baltimore, 2012)

Batey, Mavis, *Jane Austen and the English Landscape* (London, 1996)

Byrne, Paula, *Jane Austen and the Theatre* (London, 2002)

—, *The Real Jane Austen: A Life in Small Things* (London, 2013)

Copeland, Edward, and McMaster, Juliet (eds), *The Cambridge Companion to Jane Austen* (Cambridge, 1997)

Duckworth, Alistair, *The Improvement of the Estate*, new edn (Baltimore, 1994)

Fergus, Jan, *Jane Austen: A Literary Life* (London, 1991)

Fielding, Helen, *Bridget Jones's Diary* (London, 1996)

—, *Bridget Jones: The Edge of Reason* (London, 1999)

—, *Bridget Jones: Mad About the Boy* (London, 2013)

Fullerton, Susannah, *A Dance with Jane Austen* (London, 2012)

Goodwin, Alex, and Newall, Tessa, *A Guinea Pig Pride and Prejudice* (London, 2015)

Grahame-Smith, Seth, *Pride and Prejudice and Zombies* (Philadelphia, 2009)

Grey, J. David, Litz, W., and Southam, B. (eds), *The Jane Austen Handbook* (London, 1986)

Harding, D. W., *Regulated Hatred*, ed. M. Lawlor (London, 1998)

Harris, Jocelyn, *A Revolution Almost Beyond Expression: Jane Austen's Persuasion* (Newark, 2007)

Hill, Constance, *Jane Austen: Her Homes and Friends* (London, 1902)

Honan, Park, *Jane Austen: Her Life* (London, 1987)

Hubback, J. H. and E. C., *Jane Austen's Sailor Brothers* (London, 1906)

James, P. D., *Death Comes to Pemberley* (London, 2012)

Jane, Pamela, *Pride and Prejudice and Kitties* (New York, 2013)

Johnson, Claudia L., *Jane Austen: Women, Politics, and the Novel* (Chicago, 1988)

—, and Tuite, Clara (eds), *A Companion to Jane Austen* (Oxford, 2009)

Lane, Maggie, *Jane Austen's England* (London, 1986)
—, *Jane Austen and Food* (London, 1995)
Le Faye, Deirdre, *Jane Austen's 'Outlandish Cousin': The Life and Letters of Eliza de Feuillide* (London, 2002)
—, *Jane Austen: A Family Record* (Cambridge, 2004)
—, *A Chronology of Jane Austen and her Family 1700–2000* (Cambridge, 2006)
Leavis, F. R., *The Great Tradition* (London, 1948)
Lewes, G. H., 'The Novels of Jane Austen', *Blackwood's Edinburgh Magazine*, lxxxvi (July 1859), pp. 99–113.
Litz, A. Walton, *Jane Austen: A Study of her Artistic Development* (London, 1965)
Lynch, Deidre (ed.), *Janeites: Austen's Disciples and Devotees* (Princeton, 2000)
Mandal, Anthony, 'Making Austen Mad: Benjamin Crosby and the Non-Publication of "Susan" ', *RES*, ns 57 (2006), pp. 507–25
—, *Jane Austen and the Popular Novel* (Basingstoke, 2007)
—, and Southam, Brian, *The Reception of Jane Austen in Europe* (London and New York, 2007)
Mullan, John, *What Matters in Jane Austen?* (London, 2012)
Murphy, Olivia, *Jane Austen the Reader: The Artist as Critic* (Basingstoke, 2013)
Nokes, David, *Jane Austen* (London, 1997)
Percoco, Cassidy, *Regency Women's Dress* (London, 2015)
Sales, Roger, *Jane Austen and Representations of Regency England* (London, 1994)
Shepherd, Lynn, *Murder at Mansfield Park* (London, 2010)
Southam, Brian, *Jane Austen: The Critical Heritage*, 2 vols (London, 1968 and 1987)
—, *Jane Austen and the Navy* (London, 2000)
—, *Jane Austen's Literary Manuscripts*, 2nd edn (London, 2002)
Spence, Jon, *Becoming Jane Austen* (London, 2003)
Sutherland, Kathryn, *Jane Austen's Textual Lives: From Aeschylus to Bollywood* (Oxford, 2005)
—, 'Jane Austen's Dealings with John Murray and His Firm', *Review of English Studies*, 64:263 (2013), pp. 105–26
Sutherland, John, *Who Betrays Elizabeth Bennet?* (Oxford, 1999)
Tanner, Tony, *Jane Austen* (Basingstoke, 1986)
Todd, Janet (ed.), *Jane Austen in Context* (Cambridge, 2005)
—, *The Cambridge Introduction to Jane Austen*, 2nd edn (Cambridge, 2015)

Tomalin, Claire, *Jane Austen: A Life* (London, 1997)

Tucker, George Holbert, *A History of Jane Austen's Family*, rev. edn (Stroud, 1998)

Vogler, Pen, *Dinner with Mr Darcy* (London and New York, 2013)

Watt, Ian, *The Rise of the Novel* (London, 1957)

White, Gilbert, *The Natural History of Selborne*, ed. Richard Mabey (Harmondsworth, 1977)

Wiltshire, John, *Jane Austen and the Body* (Cambridge, 1992)

Winters, Ben, *Sense and Sensibility and Sea Monsters* (Philadelphia, 2009)

Websites

Jane Austen's Fiction Manuscripts: janeausten.ac.uk

Katherine Halsey, 'Jane Austen', Oxford Bibliographies Online: oxfordbibliographies.com

Persuasions: jasna.org/persuasions/on-line

The Lizzie Bennet Diaries: pemberleydigital.com/the-lizzie-bennet-diaries/

The Republic of Pemberley: pemberley.com

What Jane Saw: whatjanesaw.org